Black Americans of Achievement

LEGACY EDITION

Coretta Scott King

CIVIL RIGHTS ACTIVIST

Black Americans of Achievement

LEGACY EDITION

Muhammad Ali

Frederick Douglass

W.E.B. Du Bois

Marcus Garvey

Alex Haley

Langston Hughes

Jesse Jackson

Coretta Scott King

Martin Luther King, Jr.

Malcolm X

Thurgood Marshall

Jesse Owens

Rosa Parks

Colin Powell

Sojourner Truth

Harriet Tubman

Nat Turner

Booker T. Washington

Black Americans of Achievement

LEGACY EDITION

Coretta Scott King

CIVIL RIGHTS ACTIVIST

Lisa Renee Rhodes

With additional text written by
Dale Evva Gelfand

Consulting Editor, Revised Edition
Heather Lehr Wagner

Senior Consulting Editor, First Edition
Nathan Irvin Huggins
Director, W.E.B. Du Bois Institute
for Afro-American Research
Harvard University

CHELSEA HOUSE
P U B L I S H E R S
A Haights Cross Communications ✈ Company
P h i l a d e l p h i a

COVER: Coretta Scott King photographed in 1989.

CHELSEA HOUSE PUBLISHERS

VP, NEW PRODUCT DEVELOPMENT Sally Cheney
DIRECTOR OF PRODUCTION Kim Shinners
CREATIVE MANAGER Takeshi Takahashi
MANUFACTURING MANAGER Diann Grasse

Staff for CORETTA SCOTT KING

EXECUTIVE EDITOR Lee Marcott
ASSISTANT EDITOR Alexis Browsh
PRODUCTION EDITOR Noelle Nardone
PHOTO EDITOR Sarah Bloom
SERIES AND COVER DESIGNER Keith Trego
LAYOUT 21st Century Publishing and Communications, Inc.

Library of Congress Cataloging-in-Publication Data

Rhodes, Lisa Renee.
    Coretta Scott King : civil rights activist/Lisa Renee Rhodes, with additional text
by Dale Gelfand.
      p. cm.—(Black Americans of achievement)
Includes bibliographical references and index.
    ISBN 0-7910-8251-2 (hardcover) — ISBN 0-7910-8371-3 (pbk.)
  1. King, Coretta Scott, 1927—-Juvenile literature. 2. African American women civil rights
workers—Biography—Juvenile literature. 3. Civil rights workers—United States—Biography—
Juvenile literature. 4. African Americans—Biography—Juvenile literature. I. Gelfand,
Dale Evva, 1944- II. Title. III. Series.
E185.97.K47R564 2005
323'.092—dc22

                                                                        2004023498

Contents

Introduction   **vi**

1 Widow   **1**

2 The Scotts   **14**

3 Miss Coretta   **25**

4 Dr. and Mrs. Martin Luther King, Jr.   **37**

5 The Winds of Change   **48**

6 For Better or Worse   **63**

7 Birmingham   **72**

8 "What Are You Afraid Of?"   **84**

9 Black Madonna   **99**

10 The Dream Continues   **112**

Chronology   **120**

Further Reading   **123**

Index   **124**

About the Contributors   **136**

Introduction

Nearly 20 years ago, Chelsea House Publishers began to publish the first volumes in the series called BLACK AMERICANS OF ACHIEVEMENT. This series eventually numbered over a hundred books and profiled outstanding African Americans from many walks of life. Today, if you ask school teachers and school librarians what comes to mind when you mention Chelsea House, many will say—"Black Americans of Achievement."

The mix of individuals whose lives we covered was eclectic, to say the least. Some were well known—Muhammad Ali and Dr. Martin Luther King, Jr, for example. But others, such as Harriet Tubman and Sojourner Truth, were lesser-known figures who were introduced to modern readers through these books. The individuals profiled were chosen for their actions, their deeds, and ultimately their influence on the lives of others and their impact on our nation as a whole. By sharing these stories of unique Americans, we hoped to illustrate how ordinary individuals can be transformed by extraordinary circumstances to become people of greatness. We also hoped that these special stories would encourage young-adult readers to make their own contribution to a better world. Judging from the many wonderful letters we have received about the BLACK AMERICANS OF ACHIEVEMENT biographies over the years from students, librarians, and teachers, they have certainly fulfilled the goal of inspiring others!

Now, some 20 years later, we are publishing 18 volumes of the original BLACK AMERICANS OF ACHIEVEMENT series in revised editions to bring the books into the twenty-first century and make them available to a new generation of young-adult readers. The selection was based on the importance of these figures to American life and the popularity of the original books with our readers. These revised editions have a new full-color design and, wherever possible, we have added color photographs. The books have new features, including quotes from the writings and speeches of leaders and interesting and unusual facts about their lives. The concluding section of each book gives new emphasis to the legacy of these men and women for the current generation of readers.

The lives of these African-American leaders are unique and remarkable. By transcending the barriers that racism placed in their paths, they are examples of the power and resiliency of the human spirit and are an inspiration to readers.

We present these wonderful books to our audience for their reading pleasure.

Lee M. Marcott
Chelsea House Publishers
August 2004

Widow

Happily married to a prominent Baptist minister and civil rights leader and the mother of four beautiful children, Coretta Scott King had many blessings to count on Thursday, April 4, 1968. Still, experience had taught her to guard against being complacent about anything life had given her. Life with her husband, the Reverend Dr. Martin Luther King, Jr., had made Coretta particularly aware—at times frighteningly so—that hers would never be an ordinary family.

That spring day, however, was shaping up to be a completely uneventful one. Coretta was at home in Atlanta, Georgia, taking care of her children. As was now customary, her husband was out of town—this time in Memphis, Tennessee, where he was scheduled to lead a march to protest the unfair treatment of the city's African-American garbage collectors, who were demanding the same wages and safe working conditions as their white counterparts. Coretta and the children looked forward to spending the Easter holiday—only a few days away—with him on his return.

Coretta had even finished all of her holiday shopping, with the exception of selecting a new Easter dress for her 12-year-old daughter, Yolanda. Although she had initially had some misgivings about buying the children new clothes because she feared that the sacred meaning of the Easter holiday would be lost, she had relented to her children's entreaties, with her husband's blessing. With everything else the children faced—including long separations from their father and even bombings of their home—she had decided to spare them from feeling left out at Easter services, where everyone would be displaying their new finery.

Coretta and Yolanda went shopping in downtown Atlanta that afternoon, enjoying a pleasant mother-daughter outing. They had just come home when the telephone rang. Jesse Jackson—a young minister from Chicago and a rising voice in the civil rights movement who considered Dr. King his mentor—was on the line.

"Coretta, Doc just got shot," Jackson said. "I would advise you to take the next thing smoking."

Coretta's heart stood still as she feared the worst.

Jackson, "trying to spare me," Coretta later said, told her that Martin had been shot in the shoulder and had been taken St. Joseph's Hospital in Memphis. Coretta hung up the phone and called her best friend, Dora McDonald, to come over and be with her. She then made arrangements to catch the next plane to Memphis, which was scheduled to depart at 8:25.

A few minutes later, at about 7:15, Andrew Young, another minister, called Coretta from Memphis. Reverends Young, Jackson, and Ralph Abernathy, who had planned to take part in the protest march, had all been with Dr. King at his motel, where the shooting had taken place on the balcony. Young's news about Martin's condition was more accurate than Jackson's had been: Although Dr. King wasn't dead, he was in very serious condition with a gunshot wound to the neck. Young advised Coretta to have her friend accompany her to Memphis. Coretta decided to ask Juanita Abernathy, Ralph's wife, as well.

Coretta turned on the TV in her living room—as did millions of other Americans, who flocked to their televisions and radios to learn the details of the tragic event. The news of the shooting was almost as important to the nation as it was to Dr. King's family. For 12 years Martin Luther King, Jr., had led a nonviolent protest movement to win equal rights for black Americans and end a 400-year-old legacy of racial prejudice and injustice in the United States. African Americans were treated like second-class citizens because state and federal laws failed to guarantee them the rights enjoyed by whites, particularly in the South. A threat to Dr. King's life was a threat to the entire civil-rights movement.

The television news was reporting details of the shooting— the same details that Coretta had already heard from Young and Jackson. Suddenly, Yolanda and her younger siblings, Martin III, age 10; Dexter, 7; and little Bernice, 5, came into the living room. Coretta didn't want them to learn of their father's fate from a television report, but Yolanda had already realized that something serious had happened to her father and ran crying from the room. She returned shortly, and Coretta gathered her children around and told them the news. "I'm getting ready to go to Memphis because your daddy has been shot," she said. Yolanda, summoning up her courage, helped her mother pack her bags.

The telephone then sounded again. It was Ivan Allen, Jr., the mayor of Atlanta, who was calling to offer his help in any way. "Well, I'm leaving for Memphis on the 8:25 flight," Coretta told him. Allen immediately volunteered to escort Coretta to the airport.

Soon, other family members, friends, and neighbors were showing up at the Kings' home. Mayor Allen and his wife arrived, and Coretta kissed her children good-bye, leaving them in the care of friends, and departed for the airport, along with Dr. King's sister, Christine King Farris, and her husband, Isaac; Mayor and Mrs. Allen; and local minister Reverend Fred Bennette, Jr., and his wife. Dora McDonald would be meeting them all at the airport.

Once at the airport, Coretta hurried along the airport's corridor to find the gate for her flight, all the while feeling as though she was in a nightmare. She was about to board the plane when her name blared out over the PA system. "I had a strange, cold feeling," Coretta recalled in her autobiography, *My Life with Martin Luther King, Jr.* "For I knew that it was the word from Memphis and that the word was bad."

Mayor Allen went to the public information station for her. He returned a few minutes later, "looking grave and white." He then gave her the terrible news, confirming the worst.

"Of course I already knew," Coretta wrote, "but it had not yet been *said*. I had been trying to prepare myself to hear that final word, to think and accept it."

At 7:05 P.M., Martin Luther King, Jr., just 39 years old, had been pronounced dead at St. Joseph's Hospital. With her own 41st birthday just 23 days away, Coretta Scott King was a widow.

Coretta's tears and those of the people with her flowed unchecked. When the mayor finally asked her if she wanted to continue to Memphis, Coretta decided that her first order of business was to get home to her children.

A TEST OF STRENGTH

The ride back from the airport with the others was made in silence, although Coretta was comforted by the presence of her family and friends. She couldn't help but reflect on the coincidence of Martin's martyrdom taking place the week before Easter—which, of course, observes Jesus's death and resurrection. She recalled in her autobiography:

Although her husband's sudden death thrust multiple responsibilities onto her shoulders, Coretta's first priority was consoling her children. Here, she cradles her youngest child, five-year-old Bernice, during funeral services for Martin Luther King, Jr.

My husband had always talked of his own readiness to give his life for a cause he believed in . . . that giving himself completely would . . . [inspire] other people. This would mean the he would be resurrected in the lives of other people who dedicated themselves to a

> great cause. . . . And even in those first awful moments,
> it went through my mind that it was somehow appro-
> priate that Martin Luther King's supreme sacrifice
> should come at the Easter season.

She then turned her mind to what was most important: what to tell the children. Arriving home, Coretta found that her three youngest—Marty, Dexter, and Bernice—had been put to bed, though only Bernice was actually asleep. Yolanda was speaking to someone on the phone, but she hung up and followed Coretta as she walked to her bedroom.

"Mommy, should I hate the man who killed my daddy?" she asked.

Coretta replied, "No, darling, your daddy wouldn't want you to do that."

Going into the boys' room, she had to steel herself against breaking down when seven-year-old Dexter asked her when his daddy would return. She told her son only that his father had been badly hurt. He accepted this and went to sleep.

The night got no easier.

Dr. King's parents were devastated when they heard the news. Martin Luther King, Sr., a prominent Baptist minister and respected black leader in Atlanta, could not believe his son was dead. "I always felt I would go first," the elder King lamented to Coretta.

The King family's telephone rang continually for hours. President Lyndon Johnson called to express his condolences, as did Senator Robert Kennedy, brother of the late President John F. Kennedy. Several years before, President Kennedy and Robert Kennedy, then U.S. attorney general, had helped protect Dr. King and his followers during their protests. A phone call from Robert Kennedy back in 1960 had helped gain King's release from prison after he was arrested for refusing to give his seat to a white person at a lunch counter. (Coretta did not learn until many years later that, as attorney general,

Bobby Kennedy had reluctantly approved the request of FBI chief J. Edgar Hoover to bug Dr. King's telephones and various hotel rooms.)

Coretta knew that she had to fly to Memphis to bring her husband's body home. Senator Kennedy offered to provide a plane. He also ordered that three additional telephones be installed in the King home immediately so that Coretta and her family could respond to the flood of phone calls coming in as the news of Dr. King's death spread.

Singer and human rights activist Harry Belafonte called Coretta that night, wanting to be there for her and the children. Coretta gratefully accepted his offer. Bill Cosby and Robert Culp, then starring in TV's breakthrough interracial show *I Spy*, also flew down, helping out by playing with Dexter and Marty. Of course, thousands of strangers were also out in force, showing their love and respect for Martin Luther King, Jr.

The next day, Coretta and some friends flew to Memphis to bring home her husband's body. A huge crowd was waiting at the airport when the plane carrying Coretta and her husband's body landed back in Atlanta. Another huge crowd was assembled outside Hanley's Funeral Home, where Dr. King was taken. Coretta asked the funeral director to open the casket so that her children could see their father's body. Although the assassin's bullet had caused extensive damage to her husband's neck and jaw, as she look at him laid out in the white-satin-lined casket, Coretta thought that his face looked "so young and smooth and unworried," and the wound was barely visible. She hoped that seeing their father in his coffin would help the children—five-year-old Bernice (known as Bunny) in particular —understand that their father would not be coming home.

DEATH IN MEMPHIS

Coretta had learned the bare facts of her husband's death: Dr. King had been shot in the neck while standing on the

When Coretta brought Martin's body back to Atlanta, she wanted her children (left to right: Yolanda, Bernice, Martin III, and Dexter) to see it so that they would understand that their father would not be coming home.

balcony of the Lorraine Motel in Memphis. The assassin had fired a rifle from a room in a boardinghouse across the street from the motel. Both the Reverend Ralph Abernathy, Dr. King's closest friend and colleague, and Samuel B. Kyles, a minister from Memphis, had been with Martin on the balcony moments before his death. They were preparing to attend a local civil rights meeting with several other Southern Christian Leadership Conference (SCLC) members, including Jesse Jackson, Hosea Williams, and Andrew Young, who all waited directly below the balcony. Abernathy went back to his room to put on some aftershave; Kyles headed downstairs to the motel parking lot to join the others. When the shot rang out, they all looked up; Dr. King had fallen to the concrete floor of the balcony. Abernathy ran out of his room to see his dear friend lying in a pool of blood. Rushing over to him, he knelt beside Martin and held his head, trying to comfort him. King moved his lips, but he could not speak. One hour later, he was dead.

Leaving the funeral home to take her children home, Coretta tried to remain calm. She knew she couldn't fall apart in front of the children—but, then, it was not Coretta Scott King's nature to fall apart. She had stood bravely by her husband's side for all of the 14 years they had been married, through countless separations, numerous arrests, threatened lynchings, and even a couple of fire bombings. Their public crusade against racism had been deeply felt on both of their parts.

Like her husband, Coretta believed in nonviolence and in the right of blacks and all Americans to live in dignity and peace. Her deep religious faith had helped her face many ordeals during the struggle for civil rights. Coretta knew that justice could be won, and she understood that sacrifices were necessary to achieve it. Now her husband's life was one of those sacrifices.

MOURNING WITH THE NATION

She began to make arrangements for her husband's funeral. Four years earlier, Dr. King had won the Nobel Peace Prize for his dedication to nonviolence and his belief in the equality of all people. Coretta wanted Martin's memorial service to pay homage to his spiritual strength and moral courage.

Harry Belafonte suggested that Coretta make some sort of public statement to both comfort Dr. King's followers and answer questions from the press. He also requested her help in leading the protest march for the garbage collectors in Memphis—as her husband had intended to do—which was still scheduled for Monday, April 8. Belafonte urged Coretta to participate, telling her it would mean a lot to the movement and to the nation if she would come. Coretta knew that there was a chance of violence at the march. Her husband's death was strong evidence that deep racial hatred still existed in

America. In fact, enemies of the civil rights movement had already warned the SCLC that they would disrupt the protest march. SCLC members also worried that the demonstration would be stopped by a federal injunction. Coretta was not afraid. She agreed to go because she believed it was her duty to talk to the people and march with them. She also knew her husband would have wanted it no other way.

Coretta made the final funeral preparations. The service would take place on Tuesday, April 9—the day after the Memphis march. Dr. King's casket was placed in the Sister's Chapel at Spelman College, an all-black women's college in Atlanta, for a few days before the funeral so that people could pay their respects to the slain leader. Coretta made her speech on the Saturday before her husband's funeral. The site was Ebenezer Baptist Church, where Martin Luther King, Sr., had been pastor for more than 30 years. It was the King family's church throughout Martin's childhood, and Dr. King had eventually joined his father as its co-pastor. These strong family ties made Ebenezer the perfect place for Coretta to address Martin's followers.

"My husband faced the possibility of death without bitterness or hatred," Coretta said. "He never hated. He never despaired of well-doing. And he encouraged us to do likewise, and so he prepared us constantly for the tragedy. . . . Our concern now is that his work does not die."

Coretta thanked the SCLC, the Ebenezer Church, family, friends, and Dr. King's followers around the country and the world for their support. The leadership of the SCLC would pass to the Reverends Ralph Abernathy and Andrew Young.

On Monday, Coretta and her three oldest children flew to Memphis to lead the march for the garbage collectors. Between 25,000 and 50,000 people marched to city hall with the King family, Ralph Abernathy, and other members of the SCLC. Despite the threats, there were no disruptions or incidents of violence. Indeed, as Coretta recalled in her autobiography, "In the shock and sorrow of Martin's death the federal injunction against the march was either forgotten or rescinded; there was hardly a person in America who would have dared or even wanted to enforce it." For the entire length of the protest, both marchers and onlookers remained silent in tribute to Dr. King.

Reaching the platform at Memphis City Hall, Coretta sat with her children, looking out at the crowd. Several speeches preceded hers, and she felt that her children were comforted "to hear these good things said about their daddy." Then it was her turn to speak, and, as usual, Coretta was composed and dignified. "My spirit has been uplifted because so many thousands of persons and followers of my husband, like you, have done so many wonderful things," she said. "Your presence here today indicates your devotion." Coretta urged the people not to give up. She asked them to continue to believe in Dr. King's movement and in the principles that had guided his life. She also asked them to follow his example—to sacrifice the comforts of life for causes that would benefit all humankind. Violence had never solved any problems and it would not bring Dr. King back, she reminded the crowd.

Her words soothed the hearts and minds of the marchers, who were also inspired to see Coretta standing tall despite her tragic loss—and those who opposed the goals of the civil rights movement were given a subtle warning: Coretta Scott King was not afraid to go anywhere to spread her husband's message of love and peace. She would not be moved by threats.

SAYING GOOD-BYE

On the day of Dr. King's funeral, political, religious, and civic leaders from all over the country and people from all racial, ethnic, and economic backgrounds flocked to Atlanta's Ebenezer Baptist Church. Only a fraction of those who wanted to attend could fit into the 750-seat church, so the service was broadcast into the street over loudspeakers. Coretta— wearing a black dress, a sheer black veil, and black gloves—

The day before Martin's funeral, Coretta and her three oldest children flew to Memphis to lead the garbage collectors' march that Martin had been scheduled to lead. Between 25,000 and 50,000 people marched to city hall in what would become known as Martin's memorial march.

was unflinching. Her quiet strength was evident in the way she gently guided her children through the solemn service.

Dr. King's favorite gospel hymns filled the air. Friends gave speeches and paid tribute to his life and work. A tape of a sermon he had given at Ebenezer exactly two months before his murder, in which he prophetically talked about his own funeral, was played for all to hear. His voice both pained and soothed Coretta's broken heart.

When the funeral service was over, Coretta and her family led thousands of mourners in a march from the church to Morehouse College—the all-black men's college from which Dr. King had graduated in 1948—for a final memorial service. His casket was carried to the college on a farm wagon pulled by two mules. Coretta had chosen this method of transportation to represent her husband's dedication to the plight of the poor.

After a touching eulogy given by Martin's lifelong mentor, Dr. Benjamin Mays, Dr. Martin Luther King, Jr., was laid to rest. Coretta watched in silence as her husband's casket was placed inside a crypt deep in Atlanta's soil.

Although too busy in the months after Martin's death to be consumed by her grief, Coretta battled pain and loneliness. A few weeks after the funeral, she flew to New York to take Martin's place at a peace rally. Using notes her husband had left behind, she wrote a speech for the event. As she spoke, Dr. King's message became her own.

Coretta grieved, but her mind was set on a goal: No one would be allowed to forget the life and work of Dr. Martin Luther King, Jr. She turned her sorrow and pain into action, working tirelessly to preserve her husband's place in history as a courageous and effective activist for civil rights.

Coretta Scott King once walked the road to freedom beside her husband. Now she would walk it alone.

IN HER OWN WORDS...

The path that Coretta Scott King would take in life was in large measure directed by the racism she experienced as a child growing up in the Deep South. In her autobiography, *My Life with Martin Luther King, Jr.*, Coretta wrote:

I always smile when I hear white people talking nostalgically about the corner drugstore. I remember, when I was a very little girl, having to go to the side door of the white-owned drugstore with the other black children to buy an ice cream cone. I would have to wait until all the white children were served, and then, no matter what flavor I asked for, the man would give me whatever he had too much of. Of course, we paid exactly what the white kids paid.

The Scotts

Coretta Scott was born on April 27, 1927, in Heiberger, a small, rural hamlet in Alabama. Blacks in Heiberger and in Marion—the nearest sizeable town at 13 miles away—outnumbered whites two to one. Heiberger was a farming community, and few families worked harder at farming than the Scotts.

Coretta's grandfather, Jeff Scott, owned 300 acres of land that he shared with his children and grandchildren. (The children numbered 25 by Coretta's account. His first wife, Cora—for whom Coretta was named—gave him 13, one of whom was Coretta's father, Obadiah; after Cora's death, Jeff remarried and had 12 more kids by his second wife.) Although Coretta never met Cora, it was often said that she had inherited her grandmother's determination. Cora had helped Jeff become a prosperous farmer and an important religious and civic leader in Heiberger's large black community.

Though slavery had ended more than 50 years before Coretta's birth, the southern economy depended on cotton, and white farm owners in Coretta's hometown hired blacks to pick the crop. This photograph shows a young man harvesting cotton, much like Coretta did when she was young.

Obadiah married Bernice McMurry in 1920. Obadiah and Bernice Scott built a two-room house on the family farm, where they raised their three children in meager surroundings. Coretta, her older sister, Edythe, and her younger brother,

Obie, shared a bedroom with their parents. The children slept in one bed, Obadiah and Bernice in the other. A fireplace heated the room. The Scotts cooked meals on a wood-burning stove and got their water from a well. Their bathroom was an outhouse; the house had no running water.

Times were hard during the Great Depression, especially for blacks in the South. The Scotts were luckier than most because having a farm at least meant having food on the table. The Scotts were hardworking and devout Christians, and Obadiah Scott set a strong example for his children. He had gone from earning $3 a day working in a local sawmill when he and Bernice first got married to owning his own truck to haul logs and lumber by the time Coretta was born. A proud man, he refused to let the racism he regularly encountered break his spirit. Although Obadiah was the only black man in town who owned the truck he drove, by the time the sawmill operator had deducted what he wanted from Obadiah's pay and Obadiah had made the loan payment for his truck, little money was left to spare.

To supplement his income, he learned barbering, and customers were soon making their way to the Scott home for a trim and a shave. Whenever the line outside grew too long, Bernice helped with the haircutting.

Every Sunday, the Scotts attended Mount Tabor A.M.E. (African Methodist Episcopal) Zion Church. Grandfather Scott, a steward of the church and chairman of the board of trustees, also oversaw the Sunday-school service for children. The entire Scott clan, along with other black families from miles around, would flock to Mount Tabor to hear the Christian gospel. People came to lay down their burdens for a short while and find comfort in the church's message of forgiveness and hope. Coretta's maternal grandfather, Martin McMurry, was a singer and led the church choir and the congregation in gospel songs.

Like Grandfather McMurry, Coretta loved music. At home she listened to all kinds of records, from gospel to jazz, on her parents' big wind-up Victrola. When she wasn't listening to music, Coretta could be found playing outside with her siblings and cousins. Like other girls her age, she wore her hair in braids, but she was a tomboy underneath her feminine exterior. She enjoyed playing games, but didn't like being teased—and could put up an extraordinary fight if her brother dared to torment her. Coretta had a fiery temper. She feared no one and stood up for herself often—character traits destined to serve her well as an adult.

DEALING WITH "THE MAN"

With their father busy hauling timber all day and cutting hair evenings and weekends, it was up to the children to tend to the crops and other farming chores. "We started as soon as we were big enough to hold a hoe—I was six or seven," Coretta recalled in her autobiography. "My father hired someone to plow the fields, but we planted the corn, hoed it, and gathered it, fed the chickens and hogs, and milked the cows."

By the time she was 10, Coretta was working in the local cotton fields as well, hoeing, chopping, and picking cotton to add to the family's income. Slavery had ended more than 50 years before her birth, but the South's economy still depended on cotton, and blacks were still hired by whites to harvest the crop. "If you made five dollars in the course of the season, that was pretty good money in those Depression days," Coretta recollected. One year, Coretta managed to make an impressive $7 in the cotton fields. The extra money paid for textbooks and school supplies that fall.

Picking cotton was a symbolic reminder of the dark days of slavery, when blacks toiled in the fields for no wages. Blacks in Alabama and throughout the South continued to be degraded and victimized despite the fact that their forebears were freed—first in principle when President Abraham Lincoln signed the Emancipation Proclamation in 1863, and then in reality when the Civil War ended two years later. African

Americans were free but not equal; they still had few of the civil rights that white Americans enjoyed. If a black person was accused of a crime, a fair trial was all but impossible in a Southern courtroom. Although cases involving black defendants went to trial in accordance with the law, white judges and juries were often biased, handing down more convictions and stiffer penalties to blacks than to whites.

It was against this oppressive backdrop that Coretta's parents instilled in her the values of honesty, hard work, and thrift. The fact that their daughter was growing up at a time when stereotypes portrayed blacks as untrustworthy, lazy, and given to theft compounded the difficulty of their task.

Self-sufficient black Americans like Coretta's father were considered a threat—particularly to poor whites. Whites who had little education and struggled to make ends meet often blamed blacks for their plight. They resented any black person who lived well, regardless of how much sacrifice and hard work it had taken to do so. Rich and poor Southern whites alike commonly addressed black men as "boy" and black women as "girl." Whites—even white children—seldom called black adults by their given names. Few Southern black men would dare to look a white person in the eye or, for that matter, even walk or drive alone late at night. In the morning, he might be found dead—lynched, burned, or mutilated in some other grisly form. One of Coretta's great-uncles had been lynched and then shot to pieces by white men. (In her autobiography, Coretta marveled that her successful father "did not end up in a swamp because of his obvious self respect.") Of course, whites who lynched blacks were seldom arrested.

Grandfather Scott, who had instilled such strength in his son, could point to his own accomplishments, remarkable for a black man born just 10 years after the end of slavery and living in the hostile Deep South. He sold insurance for a living and owned an automobile. He also traveled around the country to attend important religious and civic meetings.

Grandfather Scott's and Grandfather McMurry's leadership roles in the church exemplified the type of authority that black men could hold in the South. The church was a safe haven for African Americans, one of the few places where they were shielded from insults and the threat of death. Their churches were among the few institutions in the community that blacks could own. Because most rural blacks lived in poverty, it was extremely difficult for them to become business owners. A small number of blacks were able to finish elementary and high school, and some even went on to all-black colleges or religious or liberal schools that were usually reserved for white students. These African Americans became doctors, lawyers, and teachers who provided their services to the black community.

Coretta learned about the injustice of racism in school. She and her sister, Edythe, attended a one-room elementary school—later divided into two rooms—that housed more than 100 black children in grades one through six. Instead of blackboards, parts of the walls were painted black. The unpainted wood-frame building had no indoor bathrooms, just outside toilets. Two black women taught all the students. The school had no library, and the children had to buy their own textbooks. The money Coretta and Edythe made from cotton picking was very important: They would have been unable to complete even the simplest homework assignments without the books their labor enabled them to purchase.

Every morning, no matter what the weather, Coretta and Edythe walked the three miles to school. Coretta resented the white children who would ride by on a school bus, headed for their sturdy brick building that had separate rooms for each grade, an actual library, "all sorts of equipment we never had," and even free textbooks.

The teachers at the black school inspired the Scott girls with their genuine concern for the students and their strenuous efforts to educate them despite a lack of resources. Coretta later credited one of her elementary teachers,

Mrs. Mattie Bennett, with recognizing and encouraging the sisters' eagerness to learn. Coretta was singled out to lead songs or recite poetry whenever the county supervisor came to inspect the school.

Their mother also encouraged the girls to become voracious learners. "You get an education and try to be somebody," Bernice once told Coretta. "Then you won't have to be kicked around by anybody, and you won't have to depend on anyone for your livelihood—not even on a man."

Coretta was an excellent student. Mrs. Bennett also encouraged her to develop her talent for singing by selecting Coretta to be the school's song leader. Coretta sang solos on special occasions and read poetry out loud to her classmates. When she grew older, she sang in church and performed solos in front of the congregation.

In 1938 Coretta graduated from elementary school at the top of her sixth-grade class. Edythe had graduated two years earlier and enrolled in Lincoln High School, a progressive school in Marion. Coretta followed Edythe to Lincoln High, a semiprivate school that had been started by white missionaries after the Civil War to help educate blacks. The school's founders had urged equality and social justice for all Americans, regardless of race. Lincoln's faculty was integrated—although with the exception of one Southern woman, the white teachers were from the North—but all the students were black. Although the school's tuition may not sound like much today—$4.50 per child—the Scotts had to tighten their purse strings to send their daughters to Lincoln. They knew Edythe and Coretta would benefit by learning in an environment that fostered academic and personal excellence.

Obadiah's hard work was paying off in many ways. The year before Coretta graduated from elementary school, the Scotts moved into a six-room house, complete with new furnishings. "It was the first time we had a living room and the first time my sister and I ever had a room of our own," Coretta recalled.

GOING OUT IN THE WORLD

Being able to send Edythe and Coretta to Lincoln was just one more blessing for the Scott family. Coretta's admission to Lincoln High School when she was 12 years old marked the beginning of a long journey toward personal independence and intellectual development.

Lincoln was located in Marion, 13 miles away from the Scott home. School bus service was not provided—at least not for black students; the local white kids were bused free of charge to Marion High School—so Edythe and Coretta paid to board with a black family in Marion. Living in Marion away from their parents also meant regularly interacting with whites for the first time.

Coretta flourished in school. She studied music under the tutelage of Miss Olive Williams, a black woman who had graduated from Howard University in Washington, D.C., and who specialized in classical music and voice. Although Coretta had been singing for years, both in elementary school and the church choir, she could not read music and her voice was not formally trained. With Miss Williams's guidance, Coretta learned to read music, play the piano, and sing classical works such as the *Messiah* oratorio by George Frideric Handel. She also learned to play the trumpet. Edythe, too, studied music and joined the Lincoln School Little Chorus, which traveled around the country singing in special concerts.

Coretta admired and looked up to her older sister. In many ways, Edythe was the trailblazer in the Scott family. As the oldest child, she was expected to succeed and set an example, just as her father had. Obie, a few years younger than his sisters, followed in their footsteps and also attended Lincoln.

The white teachers at Lincoln treated Edythe, Coretta, and the other students with respect, but life outside school was a different story. White youths in Marion harassed the black students as they walked to and from school. Coretta always felt uneasy when the white kids came around. She never knew what would happen. They often tried to start fights by pushing them off the sidewalk. For the most part, however, the black students refused to be bullied. Standing their ground despite taunts of "dirty niggers," they walked in a group so that no one could be singled out.

Coretta worked part-time after school cleaning house for a white woman—an experience she found troubling. The woman insisted that Coretta call her "ma'am" and that she enter the house through the back door. "I never did either," Coretta recalled. "I was not submissive enough, and I did not last long in her employment."

In 1941, the county school board finally began providing some of the cost of busing rural black students to school. Obadiah, who by this time owned three trucks, converted one of them into a school bus, and Bernice was the bus driver for the area. Coretta was now able to live at home during her junior and senior years at Lincoln. She was happy to be home. Among other things, being home gave her the opportunity to put her musical training to use. During the week, she led rehearsals for the church youth choir, and on Sundays she directed the choir and played piano during services.

RACISM STRIKES HARD

Obadiah's financial independence, his community service, and his children's accomplishments were shining examples of black achievement. This prosperity infuriated some whites in Heiberger. In the opinion of some disgruntled whites, Obadiah Scott was getting "too big for his britches."

In the fall of 1942, Edythe and Coretta were at school when the local undertaker called to tell them the bad news: Their new home—with all their beautiful new furniture—had burned to the ground. The family moved in with Grandfather McMurry, who had recently become a widower. The next day, Obadiah went to work as if nothing had happened. No one knew how the fire had started, and the police never

During Coretta's childhood, the South was a volatile place, full of racially motivated violence. This photograph shows a cross burning at a gathering of the Ku Klux Klan. Coretta would experience similar threats, including the fire at her family's home in 1942.

investigated, giving the excuse that the Scott home wasn't actually within the town.

After the fire Coretta's father seemed more determined than ever. He continued to haul timber, and by the next spring he had saved enough money to buy his own sawmill. Obadiah hired a white logger to work for him. Just a couple of weeks after being hired, the logger said that he wanted to buy the sawmill for himself, but Obadiah refused his offer. A few days later, when Obadiah went to his sawmill, he found it burned to ashes. Unbowed, Obadiah went back to hauling timber to other sawmills.

It was yet one more example to Coretta of her father's resilience, strength, and determination, which inspired and shaped her own values. In her autobiography, Coretta recalled an incident in which a white man had accused her father of still owing him $100 of unpaid debt from a car accident a couple of years earlier, in 1937. Obadiah knew that he had already met his financial obligation in the matter, but he agreed to make the payment, anyway. When he was finally out of debt, Obadiah came home from work with $40 in cash and treated his family to a shopping spree in Marion. It was not buying new merchandise but rather Obadiah's joy at once again being "a man who could run his own affairs" that was cause for celebration.

3

Miss Coretta

Antioch College, a small liberal-arts institution surrounded by the lush grass and trees of Yellow Springs, Ohio, was founded in 1852. Horace Mann, the college's first president, fought against slavery and believed that educated men and women of all races could make America a better place to live.

Edythe Scott had visited Antioch as a member of the Lincoln School Little Chorus, which performed at the college during a concert tour. In 1943, at the time of Edythe's graduation from Lincoln, Antioch decided to open its facility to black students and award scholarships to a few qualified students. The faculty and administrators had been so impressed with the quality of Lincoln's students that they contacted the school and offered one of the scholarships to its graduating students. The Scotts encouraged Edythe to apply. She was intelligent, creative, and outspoken—a strong candidate for any college—as well as Lincoln's valedictorian that year. Edythe applied, and she was

Coretta Scott as a junior at Antioch College. In her autobiography, Coretta wrote, "Antioch gave me an increased understanding of my own personal worth . . . I enjoyed a new self-assurance that encouraged me in competition with all people of all racial, ethnic, and cultural backgrounds."

awarded a one-year scholarship for tuition, room, and board, making her the "the first black student to go to Antioch on a completely integrated basis." Coretta's big sister was a pioneer.

ONWARD AND UPWARD

When Edythe won a scholarship to Antioch, the Scotts were thrilled: Their firstborn was going to college! For southern blacks, higher education was the route to personal and professional prosperity and northern institutions were deemed places where people of color could fulfill their academic promise free from the limitations and sorrows of racial discrimination. Obadiah and Bernice hoped that a college education and a chance to establish roots in the North would ensure a better life for Edythe.

Once settled at school, Edythe wrote occasional letters to Coretta, who read them with wide-eyed wonder. She learned about Antioch's open atmosphere and academic honor system. The students worked with teachers to design their own course of study, and they learned to become independent thinkers and risk takers. The faculty trusted students to make their own decisions and be responsible young adults. Antioch's beautiful campus was also a plus. "You'd love it here, Coretta," Edythe wrote.

When Coretta thought seriously about college, it didn't take her long to choose Antioch. At Lincoln she had refined her musical skills, but she looked forward to the chance to learn and do still more—especially at a college where she could be with her older sister, whom she admired very much. Not to mention it was in the North, which definitely appealed to her. Coretta applied for admission, as well as a partial scholarship, in the spring of 1945, when Edythe was a sophomore. If Coretta was accepted at Antioch, her sister could help her find her way as a college student.

To Coretta's delight, she was both accepted and awarded the $450 scholarship money to attend Antioch. Her family had to pay an additional $200 for tuition and a dorm room, plus transportation to Ohio.

NEW CHALLENGES

The fall of 1945 turned out to be a challenging one. The move from Alabama to Ohio was quite an adjustment in and of itself, but on top of that Coretta roomed with two white girls. "There was no animosity," she recalled in her autobiography, "just a matter of getting used to the situation, and eventually it worked out very well." Her studies were another matter. Coretta's first year of classes was very hard. Her study habits were not to blame; in fact, she described herself as having been a "grind"—someone who allocated little time to anything but studying. Despite her straight-A high school record, Coretta wrote in *My Life with Martin Luther King, Jr.*, that, "like most southern students, I had such an inadequate education that even Lincoln had not prepared me properly."

In her second semester at Antioch, Coretta signed up for a remedial reading class. The extra instruction helped her keep up with the grueling college curriculum. She later reflected on her eventual success, writing, "In a sense, I made more progress than some of the students who came with more advantages because I had so far to go to catch up."

In addition to completing coursework, Antioch students had to participate in the college's work-study program to graduate. Students alternated one semester of classes with a semester of work experience. At the end each work semester, every student had to write an evaluation of his or her job experience to receive a grade.

During the summer of her freshman year, Coretta worked as a junior music counselor at the Karamu Camp. The camp was operated by the Karamu House of Cleveland, an organization dedicated to bringing people of different races and ages together through music and the arts. In her sophomore year, Coretta worked for five months at the Friendly Inn Settlement House, a similar organization located in one of Cleveland's poorest neighborhoods.

Coretta broadened her study of music, adding the violin to her list of instruments. She also continued her study of music theory, voice, piano, and choral arts. She was becoming a proficient singer and musician. Walter Anderson, the only black member of Antioch's faculty, was a professor of music. He encouraged Coretta's thirst for knowledge and dedication to her craft. Jessie Treichler, a student counselor, was also fond of Coretta. Anderson and Treichler became her mentors, supporting Coretta's musical and academic efforts. Years later, Coretta recalled one of the highlights of her studies: performing in a musical program with Paul Robeson, the celebrated African-American singer and actor. Robeson was so moved by Coretta's singing that he encouraged her to continue her studies and pursue a professional career.

The academic schedule at Antioch kept students busy. In her early years at the college, Coretta was a bit shy, although all the students were polite and congenial. Coretta and Edythe were two of only six black students on campus, and Coretta felt subtle signs of prejudice among white students. "People were nice to me and tried to be friendly," she recalled years later. "But I could sense that in the back of their minds there was a feeling of race superiority bred in them through generations and by all the myths about black people they had acquired."

These subtle hints of racial inequality convinced Coretta that, despite Antioch's liberal aspirations, an invisible division existed between the few blacks and the numerous whites on campus. Years later Coretta would recall that white students considered her and her black peers to be "exceptions" to their race—rare examples of black Americans who were not as lowly as the rest. "Of course, *you're* different, Corrie," some white students would say, clearly unaware of their prejudice.

When Edythe had first enrolled at Antioch, she had shared only positive news in her letters to her younger sister, so Coretta had been unaware of any racial unease at Antioch when she applied for admission. Only after being at Antioch herself did Coretta learn that Edythe had had a difficult time being a black pioneer on a mostly white campus. Social conversations with white students always revolved around issues of race, despite the fact that Edythe, being only one person, could never speak for her entire race. In her autobiography, Coretta described Edythe as having become "awfully tired of discussing the problems of blacks at breakfast, lunch, and dinner." The social pressure Edythe felt to be "The Black Student" made it hard for her to be herself.

Nor had dating been easy for Edythe. Although young men at Antioch found the "tall and attractive" young woman an engaging lunch companion, Coretta reported that "Edythe dated white fellows on only two occasions" during her entire time at Antioch. When Coretta was a sophomore, Edythe left Antioch to enroll at Ohio State University for her senior year. The university had a larger black student population, and Edythe felt more comfortable there. Although saddened by her sister's departure, Coretta also confessed, "It was not until my sister had gone to take her senior year at Ohio State that I came into my own."

FINDING HER VOICE

Coretta declared a double major in music and elementary education in her junior year. By doing so, she became Antioch's first black education major.

The college's student-teaching program required education majors to teach for one year at Antioch's private elementary school and then for another year in the public school system. Having become primarily interested in music, Coretta decided that, for her first year, she would teach music at the Antioch school. Her second year of student teaching, though, did not go as expected: Because of her race, Coretta was barred from teaching in the Yellow Springs public schools.

Although the Yellow Springs public-school system was integrated, all the teachers were white. When the supervisor of Antioch's student-teaching program advised Coretta not to make a fuss over the issue because doing so would "imperil

Coretta went to Antioch College on the advice of her older sister, Edythe (shown here), who was a student there. Coretta later wrote that Edythe would become "awfully tired of discussing the Negro's problems at breakfast, lunch, and dinner" with her white peers while at Antioch.

the whole Antioch practice-teaching program," Coretta was outraged. How could something like this happen in a place that was supposedly racially tolerant? Coretta remembered what her father had told her whenever he was confronted by racism: "If you look a white man in the eye, he can't hurt you." She decided to fight back, making an appointment with the college president to plead her case. After listening uninterestedly to her complaint, the president replied, "Well, Corrie, what do you want us to do about it?"

Coretta suggested that the college protest the school system's decision and make an appeal on her behalf to the Yellow Springs school board. The college president refused, and Coretta was given two choices: Teach in a segregated black school in another town, or teach for another year at Antioch elementary school.

Coretta refused to teach in the segregated school, proclaiming, "I came here from Alabama to be free of segregation." Despite her hurt and disappointment, she consented to teach at Antioch's school for another year. Like her father had before her, Coretta used this painful experience to fuel her determination to excel. The episode became a turning point rather than an utter defeat. She later wrote that it also strengthened her resolve to help others:

> I said to myself, "Now, I'm going to be a Negro for the rest of my life, and I have to face these problems. So I'm not going to let this one get me down. I'll have to accept a compromise now, but I don't have to accept it as being right. I'm going . . . to do something about this situation. I don't want those who come after me to have to experience the same fate as I did."

Coretta's first step was to join the college's Race Relations and Civil Liberties committees and its chapter of the National Association for the Advancement of Colored People (NAACP). Coretta became active in campus functions that advocated the equality of all people.

As activism did, music helped soothe her spirit. In 1948 Coretta made her debut as a singer at the Second Baptist

Church in Springfield, Ohio. She would later perform there as a guest soloist. In 1950 she gave recitals in Pennsylvania and sang at her alma mater, Lincoln High School.

Antioch College showed Coretta the best of what higher education could offer as well as its serious shortcomings. She was able to take advantage of opportunities for advancement that were not commonly available to women of *any* race in the 1940s. Coretta overcame academic obstacles and blossomed into a professional singer. She also deepened her Christian commitment to helping others through community service.

Coretta also faced a deceptive form of racial prejudice and cowardice that spoiled the lives of blacks who lived in the North. Unlike the blatant racism of the South, Northern discrimination was often subtly disguised by social customs and public policies—even among people who professed liberal attitudes toward blacks. Coretta had staunchly refused to date the one black man in her college class—mainly because other Antioch students automatically saw him as her ideal escort simply because of his race. She could not stand the idea of establishing relationships with blacks only, thereby letting other people's racial assumptions determine her friends and companions. Instead, for all of her junior year she dated a white classmate. "He was Jewish, a good musician, and he had a fine mind. We had a great deal in common and we went steady for a year, until he graduated," she recalled in her autobiography.

Coretta's college experiences helped her grow stronger, wiser, and more mature. By the time she graduated from Antioch in 1951 with a bachelor of arts degree in music and elementary education, Coretta was no longer the quiet, naive young girl who had arrived from Heiberger, Alabama, on the coattails of her older sister.

"Antioch gave me an increased understanding of my own personal worth," Coretta wrote years later in *My Life with Martin Luther King, Jr.* "I enjoyed a new self-assurance that encouraged me in competition with all people of all racial, ethnic, and cultural backgrounds, on their terms or on mine."

THE HAND OF FATE

Coretta's newfound confidence helped her decide to pursue a career in music. She enjoyed teaching but felt that her true calling was to be a concert singer. Her mentor and friend Professor Anderson encouraged her to apply to the New England Conservatory of Music in Boston to continue her vocal studies. ("If it had not been for Walter, I might not have met my destiny," Coretta later wrote.) Mrs. Treichler, her counselor, helped Coretta apply for financial aid from the Jessie Smith Noyes Foundation.

Coretta was accepted at the conservatory, but the Noyes Foundation placed her name on a waiting list of students who qualified for a grant. She spent the summer of 1951 back home in Alabama with her family. The ambitious Obadiah now owned a general merchandise store, which he had purchased in 1946. Coretta had worked part-time for her father during her summers in college; now, after graduation, she again helped in the store.

By fall Coretta was ready to head to the conservatory, with or without a scholarship. She boarded a train to Boston without asking her parents to help her pay for her schooling. Coretta wanted to remain independent and took with her only the money she had saved over the summer. Meanwhile, Mrs. Treichler had made arrangements for Coretta to stay with a Mrs. Bartol. This wealthy woman gave generous donations to Antioch, and she lived in Beacon Hill, one of Boston's most affluent neighborhoods.

When her train stopped in New York, Coretta called home and learned that she had won a $650 grant from the Jessie Smith Noyes Foundation to cover full-time tuition at the New England Conservatory of Music. "My prayers had been answered!" Coretta later wrote of the news. Still, the $7 a week

Coretta as a student at Boston's New England Conservatory of Music. Life as a self-supporting woman in a large northern city was an exhilarating adventure for a girl from humble beginnings in rural Alabama.

that she agreed to pay Mrs. Bartol for housing and breakfast meant finding a job. She went through her $15 nest egg quickly once she reached Boston.

Mrs. Bartol and Coretta soon made a business deal: Coretta would help clean the fifth-floor bedrooms, halls, and stairways in exchange for her room and breakfast. The extra work relieved Coretta's financial worries to some extent, but she still had to afford her other meals and expenses. She talked Mrs. Bartol into letting her help with the laundry for extra money.

The New England Conservatory of Music was one of the top music schools in the United States. Studying there would give Coretta the chance to perfect her abilities as a concert singer in a professional setting. She hoped someday to perform with orchestras and other ensembles. Coretta was one of no more than 20 black students at the conservatory, however, and the only black living on her block in Beacon Hill. Although the social isolation was difficult, Coretta was able to handle it gracefully—thanks to her years at Antioch. She was determined not to let racial segregation stand in her way.

After several weeks in Boston, Coretta found a part-time job at a mail-order company. She couldn't have been happier with how things were falling into place. She was pursuing her professional aspirations, paying her own way, and making her own decisions. In her autobiography, Coretta's reminiscence of her first days in Boston crackle with the enthusiasm of a young woman striking out on her own. "All these years I had waited," she wrote, "and now I was here in Boston in this environment where I was absorbing music. Everything about it seemed so right."

What Miss Coretta Scott did not realize was that she was about to meet someone who would force her to rethink the future she had so carefully planned.

4

Dr. and Mrs.
Martin Luther King, Jr.

As Coretta Scott would soon learn, Martin Luther King, Jr., had his life very much in order. When he was 15 years old, Martin had begun his studies at Morehouse College, an all-black men's college in Atlanta, where he became the protégé of Dr. Benjamin Mays, a Baptist minister and the college president. Mays used the church's pulpit to denounce racial segregation and call on black men to reclaim their dignity. At 18 Martin was ordained a Baptist minister and became his father's assistant pastor at Ebenezer Baptist Church, one of the most socially progressive black churches in Georgia. Before enrolling in Boston University's School of Theology to pursue a Ph.D. in the fall of 1951, Martin had been valedictorian of his graduating class at Crozer Seminary in Pennsylvania, earning a bachelor's of divinity degree.

At just 22, therefore, Martin Luther King, Jr., was a very well educated and accomplished young man. He also had a reputation for charm and sociability, but because there weren't many young blacks in Boston, people tended to date close friends or associates. Many young adults met at church or at private parties.

Mary Powell, the wife of a nephew of Dr. Benjamin Mays, was a fellow student at the conservatory who became friends with Coretta. They had bonded because they were both older than most of the other students, 2 of only 15 or 20 black students, and had similar Southern backgrounds. Mary, who had graduated from Spelman College, knew Martin from Morehouse. The black students tended to hang out with each other, leading to occasional matchmaking. Mary, of course, mentioned Martin to Coretta.

As Coretta wrote, "The moment Mary told me the young man was a minister, I lost interest." She instantly recalled the narrow-mindedness of some ministers she had known. "Genuine piety is inspiring," she wrote in her autobiography, "but many ministers I had met went around wearing a look of sanctity that they seemed to put on like their black suits." Coretta hadn't heard about Martin's charming demeanor, however. It was true that he was a very studious minister, but he was no sanctimonious bookworm. Martin—or M.L., as friends and family called him—was known for his sense of humor and his ease in meeting new people. Still, Boston did not readily afford him the companionship of southern ladies, and he wanted to meet someone with style and charm.

When Martin asked Mary if she knew any eligible young ladies, Mary mentioned Coretta to Martin—although she had her misgivings because Coretta didn't go to church very often, so she didn't think her friend was "religious enough" for the young minister. Martin, however, was not dissuaded, and Mary finally gave in to his persistence and gave him Coretta's phone number.

A DATE WITH DESTINY

When Martin finally called Coretta at home, his wit, engaging personality, and lively conversation began to change her mind about ministers—a little bit. Martin talked about his theology studies, and Coretta talked about her music lessons. Martin was easy to talk to and didn't seem boring. He also managed to make Coretta laugh a few times, which was a good sign. He asked Coretta to lunch, and she consented. Martin agreed to pick her up the next day in front of the conservatory, playfully telling her that he would speed up the 10-minute drive and complete it in 7 just for her.

Their lunch date fell on a wet, cold January day. Coretta wore a light-blue wool knit suit and a black winter coat. "I still remember everything I was wearing that day," she later wrote. She curled her bangs, wore her hair on her shoulders, and applied a touch of lipstick. It was never her style to dress in a flashy manner.

Martin arrived at 12:00 sharp in a bright-green Chevrolet. Coretta thought he looked "short" and "unimpressive" seated behind the wheel. Although it definitely wasn't love at first sight, Coretta was open and polite. Over lunch Coretta's initial impression of Martin slowly began to change. She found him thoughtful, well spoken, and extremely intelligent. The more Coretta listened, the taller Martin seemed to become in her eyes.

Coretta was a bit nervous, but Martin's charm helped put her at ease. She talked about her own studies and offered her opinions on important social issues. Martin was not shy about his feelings on the drive back to the conservatory. He thought Coretta Scott was quite a catch and told her so. "You have everything I ever wanted in a wife," he said, citing Coretta's character, intelligence, personality, and beauty. "I want to see you again. When can I?"

Although startled by Martin's comments, Coretta played it cool. "I don't know. I'll have to check my schedule," she replied. "You may call me later."

When Coretta got home, she wasn't sure what to think. *Marriage?* She and Martin had just met! Coretta was in no rush to start a romance. In her personal affairs, Coretta had always been selective and cautious, so she was unsure about starting a relationship—especially a serious one that could lead to marriage—with Martin. Her music studies and future career came before any personal commitments. "I had thought myself in love before, but things did not work out, and I had resolved not to become emotionally entangled again until I was absolutely certain," she later remembered.

Yet Coretta knew that M.L. was very special. "With Martin I had all my defenses up, but in my heart I knew they were not too strong," she admitted. Although she feared eventually compromising her career by becoming involved with him, she also already knew that she would see him again. "I rationalized it by telling myself that he was such a fine young man, that I would wait and see what happened," she wrote in her autobiography.

THE MAN SHE WOULD MARRY

Martin Luther King, Jr., however, was a man who had never lived his life using a wait-and-see approach. Born in Atlanta on January 15, 1929, Martin seemed to possess both an adventurous spirit and a startlingly mature sense of direction from an early age. He loved to play pranks on his older sister, Christine, and younger brother, Alfred Daniel, or A.D. He was an excellent student who skipped grades 9 and 12 in high school. Despite his small stature, he was also a fierce competitor in sports and eventually played quarterback for Morehouse's football team.

Unlike Coretta, Martin hadn't known what it was like to grow up poor. His father, Martin Luther King, Sr., known as Daddy King, was a Baptist minister and self-made business-man who had risen from poverty to a solidly middle-class standard of living. Martin Sr. had married Alberta Williams in November 1926, and when Alberta's father, also a minister, died suddenly five years later, she inherited her father's 12-room house. Furthermore, Martin Sr. took over his father-in-law's

Martin Luther King, Sr., known as Daddy King, was a highly respected minister and advocate in the black community. When Coretta first met him, he extolled the virtues of other girls his son had been interested in, saying, "Those girls have a lot to offer." In the end, though, he gave Martin and Coretta his blessing.

pastoral duties of Ebenezer Baptist Church. Reverend King became an outspoken advocate for the rights of southern blacks, even leading a voter registration drive in 1935. By the time his children were born, Reverend King was highly respected in the black community.

The childhood experience that Martin and Coretta did have in common was racism—and the determination to rise above it. Atlanta wasn't exempt from segregation, and Martin attended a segregated elementary school while his white neighborhood playmates went to school elsewhere—after which they were forbidden by their parents from further association with a "colored boy." Once, Martin's father refused to buy shoes at a white-owned store because a clerk told him to sit in the back to be served. Daddy King stormed out, dragging young M.L. by the hand and vowing never to accept such treatment quietly.

Years later Martin recalled his growing up with "a sense of somebodiness." Like Obadiah and Bernice Scott, the Kings had instilled an unshakable sense of self-confidence in their children. Martin never saw his parents weaken under the weight of racism.

In *My Life with Martin Luther King, Jr.*, Coretta recalled learning that Martin found the purpose of his ministry after attending a lecture about the life of Mahatma Gandhi, who had led the people of India in nonviolent protests against the then-ruling British government. This small, thin, bespectacled man became a powerful, towering figure by spreading his belief that freedom and social justice could be won in India using love, self-sacrifice, and truth as weapons. Martin had been so moved by Gandhi's philosophy that he read every book he could find on the subject and immersed himself in Gandhi's doctrine of *satyagraha* ("force born out of truth")— the belief that government oppression could be stopped by nonviolent citizen boycotts, strikes, and marches. Satyagraha complemented Martin's belief in Christianity and in Jesus's peaceful example of facing evil and overcoming enemies.

CONNECTING

Coretta also quickly learned that, although Martin felt a deep desire to use his gifts to serve God, he didn't want to fulfill his life's mission alone. He longed for a wife and family. She was hardly surprised, then, when she got another call from Martin the day after their lunch date, suggesting that they get together that Saturday night. Coretta already had both plans to attend a small party and an escort. She told Martin that he was welcome to come with her if her escort could not make it—which turned out to be the case.

Coretta went to the party on the arm of Martin Luther King, Jr. Other young women at the party fawned over her date, but she pretended to be oblivious to their "swooning"—and to Martin's pleasure in it. To herself, however, she admitted, "There [was] no question in my mind that he was the most eligible young black man in the Boston area at that time."

They were equally smitten. The couple shared long walks and conversation—Coretta was impressed by the breadth of his knowledge—and socialized at small dinner parties. They also went dancing and attended concerts together. Martin's intention to marry Coretta became unmistakably clear. There was only one problem: He was already informally engaged to a young woman in Atlanta. The engagement had been set up by the couple's respective families with Martin Sr.'s approval. Martin had little interest in marrying a woman who had been handpicked for him, but he also had a difficult time defying his father's wishes.

Coretta knew about the engagement and Martin's reluctance to approach his father. She wasn't in a hurry to decide her fate, though. Coretta desperately wanted to continue her studies; she also still preferred to marry someone other than a minister—and although Martin greatly admired Coretta's musical talent and her intellectual pursuits, he made it clear that he wanted a mate whose primary role would be wife and mother.

By the summer of 1952, Coretta had grown to love Martin. When her sister came to Boston to meet him, she gave Coretta the nod of approval. In fact, Edythe eventually helped Coretta make up her mind about Martin, telling her that, if she married him, she might not have the professional singing career she had so long envisioned, but she would certainly not be without a career. Coretta, however, was determined to complete her studies at the conservatory, regardless of Martin's intentions.

That summer, Coretta visited Atlanta to meet the King family, staying with Mary Powell, who had gone home for summer break. Reverend and Mrs. King were polite, but they didn't make any grand overtures to their son's new love interest. After all, Martin was still "engaged." Coretta took the tension in stride. She visited Ebenezer Church and was impressed by both Martin's sermons and his compassion. Still, she resisted making a decision.

That fall the Kings came to Boston. Coretta listened politely as Martin Sr. listed the fine points of all the Atlanta girls whom Martin been involved with briefly and then lost interest in, particularly extolling the virtues of the girl they had chosen for him. "Those girls have a lot to offer," Martin Sr. declared. Hearing how wonderful all his previous girlfriends were rankled Coretta, who countered, "I have something to offer, too."

Soon after—perhaps buoyed by the courage of his intended —Martin told his father that he planned to finish his doctoral studies in Boston and marry Coretta Scott. By Christmas the Kings were convinced that Martin and Coretta would be husband and wife. Daddy King finally gave them his blessing.

A LIFE TOGETHER BEGINS

Coretta began to make wedding plans. She decided to change her major at the conservatory to music education and voice. This degree would enable her to teach for a living as well as perform professionally. She had decided, "Regardless of what happens after I marry Martin, I will adjust myself to these conditions, whatever they may be."

Perhaps surprisingly, she still hadn't made her "final judgment" about whether marrying Martin was the right decision. "[E]verything pointed in that direction," she later recalled, "but I still was not sure."

Nonetheless, Coretta Scott and Martin Luther King, Jr., were married on June 18, 1953, on the lawn of the Scott family's new home, which Obadiah had built the next to his general store in Marion. The wedding was small, and Coretta opted for a pale-blue ankle-length gown rather than a customary white one. Martin Sr. performed the wedding ceremony. At the request of his son and daughter-in-law, Daddy King omitted the traditional bride's vow to "obey" her husband.

The newlyweds spent their honeymoon in Alabama at a family friend's home—which also happened to be a funeral parlor. The young couple had no other choice because blacks were not allowed to stay at white-owned hotels or motels. Although the reason behind their somewhat strange choice of bridal suite was painful, the couple's honeymoon in a funeral parlor eventually became a source of a shared joke between them.

The Monday after her wedding, Coretta took a summer job in Atlanta, clerking for a bank that Daddy King helped run. She and Martin stayed with the Kings until fall, when they returned to Boston to complete their degrees. Coretta crammed her schedule with 13 courses, including lessons for voice and several instruments. She also worked in another student-teaching program and performed in several recitals.

During their first year of marriage, Coretta and Martin shared household chores, cooking, and grocery shopping because her course load was so heavy. Martin made it clear, however, that he was the head of the household. Coretta wrote about one notable instance of him asserting his authority. On this occasion her young husband said, "I want my wife to respect me as the head of the family. I am the head of the family."

Coretta wrote, "We laughed together at that slightly pompous speech, and he backed down. 'Of course, I don't really mean that,' he said. 'I think marriage should be a shared partnership.'" Coretta was insightful enough to know that part of Martin really *did* mean it and that she would have to seriously adjust to married life. She felt strongly that it was important to retain some independence, and she still hoped someday to be a concert singer. In the years to come, Coretta

Martin and Coretta were married on June 18, 1953, on the lawn of the Scott family's new home. In this photograph, the couple is shown emerging from a courthouse where Martin had been tried for conspiracy to boycott. It would be one of many tests of their marriage.

would nurture her family while also using her creative talents outside the home as a singer and a teacher. To support his wife's aspirations, Martin would later purchase a piano for her so that she could continue playing.

While the couple lived in Boston, Martin preached at local churches to help pay expenses. This experience led Martin to think about beginning a ministry in the South. "I preach because I can't help myself," he told Coretta. Coretta could not have foreseen the changes to her life that would come as a result of her husband's seemingly simple dream.

5

The Winds of Change

The South's racially unjust traditions and laws were held up to public scrutiny in the spring of 1954. On May 17, the United States Supreme Court, ruling on a case called *Brown* v. *Board of Education of Topeka, Kansas*, declared that educational facilities that kept blacks separate from whites were "inherently unequal." The court's decision meant that the federal government could no longer sanction the legal separation of blacks and whites in public schools. In 1955 the Court ordered the states to desegregate their public education systems "with all deliberate speed."

The tradition that Coretta, Martin, and hundreds of thousands of other southern blacks had grown up with—separate schools for each race—was now illegal. The court's decision was the first step in ending racial segregation throughout the country, although the effect was felt primarily in the South.

Brown v. *Board of Education* was a huge moral and social victory for southern blacks. The NAACP Legal Defense and Education Fund had tried for more than 10 years to convince southern courts that laws permitting the separation of blacks from whites in public life were against the legal and moral principles of the Fourteenth Amendment to the U.S. Constitution, which guarantees all Americans equal protection under the law, regardless of race. Thurgood Marshall, a brilliant black lawyer and director of the NAACP Legal Defense Fund, had led—and ultimately won—the battle against segregation in public schools. It finally seemed as if African Americans could rely on the highest court in the land to guarantee and defend their rights.

BACK TO HER ROOTS

For Coretta and Martin, the legal end of segregation coincided with a new beginning in one of the most racially divided cities in the nation: Montgomery, Alabama. During the Civil War, Montgomery had been known as "The Cradle of the Confederacy"; as late as the 1950s, blacks and whites could be arrested for socializing together in public.

Coretta had recently graduated from the New England Conservatory of Music and Martin was finishing his doctoral dissertation when Martin was offered the pastoral seat at Dexter Avenue Baptist Church in Montgomery. He couldn't refuse the challenge. Martin hoped he could inspire the middle-class, well-educated congregants to have more involvement with the entire black community. If he could motivate the people, he could then put his beliefs about nonviolence and social justice into practice. Dr. King also dreamed of having a congregation made up of both blacks and whites from all social classes.

Coretta had serious reservations about returning to the South. "I wanted to breathe the freer air and the richer cultural life of the North a while longer and to enjoy the greater opportunities a northern city would give me for furthering my musical career," she recalled in her autobiography. A major legal milestone against segregation may have been won, but racism was still a fact of life in the South.

Martin, however, felt an urgent need to pastor at a southern black church, so Coretta decided to make the best of the

Brown v. Board of Education

"All men are created equal." This is perhaps most famous phrase in the Declaration of Independence, written by Thomas Jefferson in 1776. In practice, however, that phrase generally applied only to whites. Education was no exception.

Until 1954, many schools in the United States—especially in the South—had their own interpretation of the Fourteenth Amendment, which rules that "No state shall make or enforce any law which shall abridge the privileges or immunities of citizens of the United States, nor shall any state deprive any person of life, liberty, or property. . . ." Those who backed segregated schools argued that "separate but equal" educational facilities for whites and blacks did not violate the Fourteenth Amendment. This "separate but equal" doctrine had been established by the 1896 Supreme Court case of *Plessy* v. *Ferguson.*

The case of *Plessy* v. *Ferguson* involved a 30-year-old black shoemaker named Homer Adolph Plessy, who had been jailed for sitting in a "white" car on the East Louisiana Railroad. Plessy, who was only one-eighth black, was considered "colored" by Louisiana state law and therefore was required to ride in the "colored" car. Plessy sued the state of Louisiana in a case heard by Judge John Ferguson. When Plessy lost, he appealed first to the Louisiana Supreme Court and then to the U.S. Supreme Court. The Court upheld Judge Ferguson's ruling, decreeing that the separate facilities the railroad had provided were constitutional as long as they were equal. Thus the "separate but equal" policy came to include restaurants, theaters, and, of course, public schools.

The historic ruling of *Brown* v. *Board of Education* came about as a result of a lawsuit brought by the parents of Linda Brown, an eight-year-old black child from Topeka, Kansas. They felt it unjust that their child was forced to cross the city to attend school while her white playmates could attend the public school just a couple of blocks away.

situation. By the end of the summer, they had moved into their new house Montgomery. She quickly made friends with Juanita Abernathy, the wife of Ralph Abernathy, a young, outspoken black minister who pastored at the First Baptist Church in Montgomery.

The federal district court sided with the school district, saying that as long as blacks and whites had schools that were basically the same, black students were being treated equally with whites according to the Fourteenth Amendment.

The Browns weren't satisfied with the ruling, and their lawyers fought on with the encouragement of the NAACP, whose chief counsel, Thurgood Marshall, eventually argued the case before the Supreme Court. (Marshall, the grandson of slaves, became the first black Supreme Court justice. He was appointed to the bench in 1967 and served for 24 years.)

The issue before the court was this: Does racial segregation of children in public schools deprive minority children of equal protection of the laws under the Fourteenth Amendment? The court decided that it did:

> We come to the question presented: Does segregation of children in public schools solely on the basis of race, even though the physical facilities and other "tangible" factors may be equal, deprive the children of the minority group of equal educational opportunities? We believe that it does.
>
> Segregation of white and colored children in public schools has a detrimental effect upon the colored children. The impact is greater when it has the sanction of the law, for the policy of separating the races is usually interpreted as denoting the inferiority of the Negro group. A sense of inferiority affects the motivation of a child to learn. Segregation with the sanction of law, therefore, [impedes] the educational and mental development of Negro children and [deprives] them of some of the benefits they would receive in [an integrated] school system. . . . We conclude that, in the field of public education, the doctrine of "separate but equal" has no place. . . .

The decision was a profound one. This one ruling spelled the beginning of the end of legal segregation of all public facilities in the United States.

Martin preached every Sunday, often turning to Coretta for sermon ideas before putting pen to paper, and he traveled back and forth to Boston to finish his thesis. He was finally awarded his Ph.D. in June 1955. Coretta was almost as busy as her husband. Her musical gifts and training served her well as a soloist and helper in Dexter Avenue Baptist's choir. A few months after settling in Montgomery, she also performed in a concert in Georgia, and in early 1955, she sang in two concerts. She stopped performing that spring, after discovering that she was pregnant. "Martin was, if anything, happier about this than about his degree," Coretta wrote. Her pregnancy was particularly rewarding because they had had some doubt about whether they could conceive.

Coretta gave birth to her first child, Yolanda Denise (whom they called Yoki), on November 17, 1955. She came home from the hospital a week after the baby was born, looking forward to a quiet time with her new daughter and getting used to motherhood. The winds of change began to blow hard in the South just two weeks after Yoki's birth, however. The turbulence began with a simple act of defiance.

STANDING UP BY SITTING DOWN

On December 1, 1955, Rosa Parks, a 42-year-old black seamstress at a local department store, was riding a crowded city bus home from work. At that time, blacks had to sit in the back of buses. If no seats were available in the black section, black passengers had to stand—regardless of how many empty seats there were in the white section. Furthermore, if all the seats in the white section were occupied, black passengers had to give up their seats to white passengers. (The ultimate insult: After black passengers boarded the bus in the front to pay their fare, they had to get off the bus and walk to the rear door and reboard in "their" section.) That's exactly what happened to Rosa Parks. Parks, however, refused to give up her seat. She had put in a long day at work, she had paid the same fare as the

After some doubt about whether they could conceive, Coretta discovered that she was pregnant in the spring of 1955. The couple would go on to have four children, three of whom (left to right: Martin III, Yolanda, and Dexter) are shown here.

white passengers, and she was tired of how the Montgomery City Bus Lines harassed and insulted blacks. The bus driver told her to stand or be arrested, but Parks steadfastly remained seated. She was apprehended by police and taken to jail.

News of her arrest spread through the black community like wildfire. Historian David Garrow wrote in his book

Bearing the Cross that E.D. Nixon, a former president of the local NAACP, decided with several black community leaders, including Ralph Abernathy, to organize a black boycott of Montgomery buses to protest the arrest and to push political leaders to make the city's segregation laws more equitable. An organization would be formed to lead and sustain the bus boycott until the segregation law was defeated. Abernathy suggested that the group be called the Montgomery Improvement Association (MIA) and that Martin Luther King, Jr., be its leader.

The boycott was set for the following Monday, December 5 —the day of Mrs. Parks's trial. Martin and the other leaders spent that weekend distributing leaflets to the more than 50,000 blacks who lived in Montgomery, explaining the boycott's importance. Black-owned taxi companies were asked to provide group rates for blacks commuting to and from work. Everyone was urged to stay off the city buses. Coretta manned the phone all weekend, fielding calls from community leaders and citizens who wanted updates and helping coordinate volunteer car pools.

Come Monday morning, Coretta was up and dressed by 5:30 A.M., eager to see the boycott in action. The King home happened to be located on the corner with a bus stop for one of the busiest lines in the city. The first bus of the day would arrive at 6:00. Coretta had toast and coffee as she waited.

The bus arrived on schedule—empty! Not a single passenger was on board. Coretta called Martin to the window as the bus rolled away. They went outside to await the next one; it was also empty, as were several others that followed.

Similar scenes were taking place throughout the city. Boycotters walked, rode in taxis, or pedaled bicycles. A few mules and horse-drawn buggies were even seen plodding along the streets of Montgomery. People simply found other ways to get to and from work. The city's black residents were determined make their discontent known.

At 9:00 Martin and Abernathy arrived at the city court-house for Mrs. Parks's trial. The judge ruled that she had violated a state segregation law and fined her $10. When her lawyer, Fred D. Gray, filed an appeal, the legal battle over Montgomery's segregation laws began. One act of defiance had given birth to the civil-rights movement.

THE BEGINNING OF AN ERA

An organization was soon formed to lead and sustain the bus boycott until the segregation law was defeated. Martin reluctantly accepted the post of president. Despite the potential danger to her family in his taking on leadership of a civil-rights group in such a racist climate, Coretta supported his decision, saying, "You know that whatever you do, you have my backing."

Five thousand people turned up at the Holy Baptist Church to hear a speech by the new leader of the boycott movement. Martin called on the people to find the faith and the courage to protest with dignity. "This is our challenge and our over-whelming responsibility."

The black community agreed and pledged to support the boycott's three demands: The harassment of black bus passengers was to end; the bus companies were to adopt a first-come first-served seating policy, with blacks taking seats from the back of the bus forward and whites from the front moving backward; and black bus drivers were to be hired to drive city bus routes that served black neighborhoods.

The bus companies refused to bargain, so the boycott continued. By mid-December the MIA had to organize numerous volunteer car pools to take blacks to and from work. The King home became MIA headquarters, and Coretta answered telephone calls, coordinated car pools, and updated boycotters on the ongoing schedule of community meetings. All the while she cooked and cared for her husband and baby daughter—along with the numerous people whom her husband often invited to stay for dinner. "Sometimes it seemed like a loaves-and-fishes miracle," she recalled in her autobiography.

Coretta found the boycott inspiring and was heartened that the "Movement," as she called it, seemed to be spreading out across the entire country—and beyond. "We began to see that it was not only a national but an international phenomenon, part of a worldwide revolution of humanity, asserting the individual's right to freedom and self-respect." She was thrilled to be a part of it.

Coretta worked tirelessly to keep the boycott going. Her primary responsibility was to help people find rides to and from their jobs. She recalled in her autobiography, "With all we could do, thousands of people still had to walk. They walked magnificently and proudly. Somebody asked one old grand-mother, coming down the street, if she was not tired. She answered, 'It used to be my soul was tired and my feets rested; now my feet's tired, but my soul is rested.'" She was also amused by the inadvertent support of the boycott by white employers. "Without meaning to, some white women helped us by driving down to pick up their black maids, to make sure they got to work."

THE ATTACKS BEGIN

Many whites were furious at the success of the boycott. Further-more, many racists resented the Kings for being "uppity" blacks who needed to be taken down. Coretta and Martin began receiving obscene and threatening phone calls.

In January 1956 the harassment took a new turn when Dr. King was arrested for a minor traffic violation—ostensibly doing 30 in a 25 mile-per-hour zone. After refusing to release him when Ralph Abernathy offered to post bail, Martin's jailers relented when a crowd started gathering.

Soon after, the abusive phone calls began increasing. On one day alone, 30 to 40 disturbing phone calls were made to the Kings' home. Coretta soon found it necessary to take the phone off the hook for several hours each night—which, of course, interfered with her work for the boycott. The Kings' primary fear, however, was being firebombed. Other bombings had occurred in rural areas outside the city; even though the Kings lived in a densely populated area, they worried that their home would be targeted. On January 30, 1956, the Kings' worst nightmare came true. While Martin was giving a speech at Ralph Abernathy's church, Coretta and Mary Lucy Williams, a friend from Dexter Avenue Church, heard a loud thump on the porch of the Kings' home. It was 9:30 P.M. Mentally prepared for the possibility of an attack, Coretta reacted swiftly. "It sounds as if someone has hit the house. We'd better move to the back," she instructed her terrified friend.

Dressed in her bathrobe, Coretta started to lead Mary Lucy to the back bedroom, where Yoki was sleeping in her bassinet, when a blast shook the house and filled the air with smoke and flying glass. Grabbing her terrified friend, Coretta hustled her to the Kings' bedroom and made sure that her daughter was unharmed. Coretta then grabbed the telephone. As she recalled in her autobiography, she suddenly felt uneasy about calling the police. Instead, she called the church where her husband was speaking.

Martin rushed home to find the living room windows smashed, the front porch split in half, and the lights blown out. His family was safe, though. The Kings' neighbors had already gathered to see if they could help. The mayor and the police commissioner also came, as did several white reporters. Several black neighbors, outraged and anxious to retaliate for the bombing, clashed with the police officers on the scene. Martin defused this potentially explosive situation, exhorting his supporters to "meet violence with nonviolence." The crowd slowly dispersed, and Coretta recounted how a white cop was heard to say, "If it hadn't been for that nigger preacher, we'd all be dead."

The bombing did not break the young couple's resolve to continue leading the boycott. Shortly after the explosion, both Obadiah Scott and Daddy King made desperate bids to take Coretta and their granddaughter back to the safety of either Marion or Atlanta. Coretta declined, saying, "I would not be satisfied if I went home. I want to be here with Martin." Coretta and Martin returned to their house in Montgomery as soon as it was repaired, installing outside floodlights. The congregation insisted on hiring an unarmed night watchman for extra protection.

When Martin told his wife that he didn't know what he would have done if it hadn't been for her, Coretta was deeply affected by the praise. "I had always been a strong person," she later wrote, "but I had not realized that Martin, so strong himself, did need me."

Several days after the bombing, Coretta silently reflected on the threat to her family. She found the experience surprisingly enlightening. Coretta finally realized why she had married

IN HER OWN WORDS...

After their house was firebombed, Coretta felt a new sense of determination, resolve, and faith. She noted in her autobiography how excited she was to participate in the groundswell that was shaking up the status quo:

I was excited about all that was going on, and I felt that I was a part of it. I was making a contribution. Something was moving, evolving, going in a direction that we could not control. We started out with a one-day protest. Because of the resistance that we faced, it got longer and longer. Finally, when we realized that those in charge weren't willing to give in at all, we decided to go all out for integration. We did not know what the end would be, but we knew that there was going to be a continuation and that in many ways we were fortunate and blessed to have been chosen to be part of what was taking place. We felt as if we were being directed and guided.

Coretta jubilantly greets Martin after leaving the courthouse in Montgomery, Alabama. "I felt there was a larger force working with me and that I was not alone," she would later reflect about her marriage to Martin. "I knew at that point that being with him . . . was the right thing for me."

Martin. "I felt there was a larger force working with me and that I was not alone," Coretta recalled years later. "I knew at that point that being with him, and participating in the Movement, was the right thing for me." Coretta's hope of returning to the North was replaced by a deep commitment to the fight against social injustice. She would never again question her mission in life.

THE BATTLE RAGES ON

After three months the boycott was still going strong, and city officials fumed. To end it, the city found an obscure law against boycotting on its books and then charged about 90 of the bus protest's leaders with a violation. Martin, who was on a lecture tour when the arrests began, canceled his speaking engagements and hurried to Atlanta, where Coretta and Yoki were visiting with Mamma and Daddy King. Martin knew he would be arrested immediately on his return to Montgomery, but he resolved not to desert his people. Nonetheless, his mother and father did their best to convince him not to go back.

Coretta—feeling strongly now that she and her husband had been "chosen" to be part of the civil rights movement—weighed in with her own opinion, her newfound sense of purpose resonating in every word:

> Martin, there comes a time in every person's life when he has to make a decision all by himself, when he has to stand alone. This is such a time in your life. You know that what you feel is right, and I want you to know that whatever you decide to do, I will always be with you.

The next morning, accompanied by Ralph Abernathy (who had previously been arrested and released on bail) and Daddy King, Martin turned himself in at the Montgomery courthouse. His trial began on March 19, 1956. Four days later, the judge found him guilty and sentenced him to pay $500 or serve 386 days of hard labor. Martin's lawyers appealed the decision.

The wheels of justice had been grinding for months in the lawsuit that community leaders had filed after the arrest of Rosa Parks to question the legality of Alabama's segregation laws. In June a federal court ruled that the laws were unconstitutional, but the city's lawyers appealed the case to the Supreme Court. The boycotters continued to protest—and waited.

By this time Martin Luther King, Jr., was becoming a national figure, even a household name. Newspaper and television reporters from around the country traveled to Alabama to cover the pending appeal, and black and white activists and lawyers from both the South and the North came to Montgomery to help map out strategies to sustain the boycott.

The boycott continued through the fall, and by then black participants were being harassed more than ever. Boycotters were pulled out of cars and beaten. Black-owned gas stations were bombed, further hampering the car pools. Even walking to work involved a high risk of bodily harm for the protesters. It was becoming more difficult for the leaders to maintain their morale. Coretta continued to coordinate the boycott from the Kings' home, but the project was losing steam.

Then in late October 1956, the Montgomery city government went to court to get an injunction to stop carpooling in black communities, claiming that the car pools were a "public nuisance" that compromised the quality of life in the city. The boycott was now in serious danger.

Coretta took an optimistic attitude. She told her husband, "You know, what I think is going to happen is that by the time they get this injunction, the Supreme Court will have ruled for us. I think everything is going to work out all right." Coretta later admitted in her autobiography that she wasn't even sure she believed this optimistic forecast herself.

A CHANGE IS GONNA COME

On November 13, 1956, Coretta and Martin were sitting in the courtroom waiting for the judge to decide the case. Suddenly, the mayor and police commissioner got up, as did the city attorneys. A general hubbub began, and one of the reporters came over and handed Martin a piece of paper. Coretta related that her husband's face was "beaming" as he read the note aloud, stating that the United States Supreme Court had just declared Alabama's state and local laws that required segregation on buses unconstitutional. The legal battle that had begun with Rosa Parks was finally over. The boycotters had won.

Coretta celebrated the historic occasion in a very special way. On December 5, 1956, the first anniversary of the boycott, she performed in a concert at the Manhattan Center in New York to raise funds for the MIA. The featured act on a list that included such luminaries as Duke Ellington and close family friend Harry Belafonte, Coretta sang a program of classical music plus an original composition that told the story of the bus boycott. She had interwoven spoken narrative with gospel songs to convey the struggle for freedom throughout history.

Coretta was jubilant that night. Describing the bond she forged with her audience, she later wrote, "I could feel the warm responsive love between us." This was one time Coretta was glad she had never given up on her dream to become a concert singer.

On December 20 a long-awaited dream of Montgomery's black community also came true: The U.S. Supreme Court ruling to desegregate the city's buses went into effect. The mayor declared that the bus companies would obey the ruling, and the police would cooperate.

The next morning Martin, Ralph Abernathy, and MIA Treasurer E.D. Nixon rode with Rosa Parks aboard the first desegregated bus on the South Jackson Avenue line. After 382 long days of nonviolent protest, change was slowly coming to Montgomery, Alabama.

6

For Better or Worse

Such radical change didn't happen smoothly. The newly integrated buses were stoned and shot at. Racist mobs dragged blacks off buses and even shot a pregnant black woman in her leg. Nor were the leaders of the movement ignored. The Kings escaped injury when someone fired a gun though their front door. Ralph Abernathy's house and church were both dynamited. Three other churches were bombed, as well. The violence came to a head the night of January 28, when 14 sticks of smoldering dynamite landed on the Kings' front porch.

Finally even the white citizens of Montgomery had had enough. Government officials as well as a group of leading businessmen denounced the attacks, newspaper editorials railed against the violence, and a group of ministers called for "peaceful acceptance of desegregation." The violence ended. Now there would be no turning back in the fight for civil rights.

WITNESS TO HISTORY

Coretta was now the wife of the most newsworthy black leader in America. Blacks and whites alike wanted to know more about the dynamic young southern preacher who was managing to turn the entrenched racist South upside down with a fervent nonviolent protest movement. The Montgomery Improvement Association maintained contact with scores of newspaper reporters who came to Montgomery to record the ongoing events.

Montgomery was just the tip of the iceberg. Inspired by the success of the boycott, other organizations in other southern cities were starting their own movements. Black ministers throughout the South began to follow the MIA's example, organizing their congregations to fight racial injustice. Bayard Rustin, a civil-rights and peace activist and a fellow follower of Gandhi's philosophy who had become Martin's friend, convinced Martin that all the protest groups should be brought together into one national organization. Agreeing, Martin organized a meeting to be held at Daddy King's Ebenezer Baptist Church in Atlanta.

It so happened that the night before the meeting was the same night that Montgomery's black community was besieged by a sudden rash of church firebombings—including that of Ralph Abernathy's church. Martin asked Coretta to take his place at the meeting the next day, January 10, so that he and Abernathy could return to Montgomery to help the community cope.

Coretta was the meeting's first speaker. She presented the MIA's plan for building a southern coalition to direct the protest movement. The gathering of ministers and civic leaders unanimously supported the plan. Thus, the Southern Christian Leadership Conference (SCLC) was born. The organization's headquarters was established in Atlanta. Martin was elected president.

As soon as the SCLC was established, the organization sent President Dwight Eisenhower the second of two messages, asking him to investigate racial injustice in the South and to respond to the terrorist attacks that had followed the Montgomery boycott. The White House remained silent.

That spring Coretta and Martin traveled to the West African nation of Ghana for ceremonies that would mark the country's independence from Britain and its emergence as a new nation. At midnight on March 7, the new government, headed by a black man, Kwame Nkrumah, took power. To the sound of bells tolling, the British flag was lowered over Parliament House and the new flag of Ghana was raised. Coretta recalled in her autobiography, "It was an immensely thrilling moment for Martin and me. We felt a strong sense of identity and kinship with those African people shouting 'Freedom!' in their different tongues. We were so proud of our

The Right to Vote

Although technically black men had been granted the right to vote with the passage of the Fifteenth Amendment in 1870, in actuality laws called "grandfather clauses" prohibited blacks from voting if their grandfathers—most of whom had been slaves—could not register to do so. Further, most southern states had laws that required blacks to pay as much as $2 to vote—the so-called poll tax—plus back taxes for every year they had not voted since age 21. Even more discriminatory, blacks in some states had to pass difficult literacy tests that asked questions about law and history—and even if they managed to pass, the white bureaucrats in charge would flunk them. Needless to say, none of these restrictions applied to whites. They were strategically designed to prevent blacks—especially the poor and undereducated—from exercising their rights as citizens.

On May 17, 1957, more than 30,000 people marched to the steps of the Lincoln Memorial to hear Martin Luther King, Jr., demand the ballot for blacks. The pilgrimage marked the launch of a massive voter education and registration drive throughout the South. The goal was to register 5 million new black voters. At that point, in all the southern states, only 1.25 million blacks were registered.

African heritage and saw in Ghana a symbol of the hopes and aspirations of all our people."

The Kings continued to Nigeria and then visited Italy, Switzerland, France, and Great Britain. Rome was a particular favorite of Coretta's; she enjoyed both the "friendly warmth of the Italian people and the feeling of going back into history and seeing the events [I] had read about come alive."

It was a very happy time for Coretta and her family, one made even happier by her second pregnancy.

A FAITH IS TESTED

Over the next year, Coretta barely saw Martin as he fought for equality in the voting booth. *Jet* magazine calculated that Martin had delivered 208 speeches and traveled 780,000 miles. "It certainly seemed so to me," she recalled a bit wistfully. He did manage to be home on October 23, 1957, when Coretta gave birth to their first son, Martin Luther King III. Her husband was "ecstatic." With Marty's birth Coretta's responsibilities multiplied, but she still juggled everything in her life with grace and efficiency.

In the spring of 1958, Coretta packed her bags and hit the road to make her official debut as a public speaker. The New Hope Baptist Church in Denver had invited her to be the guest speaker for its Women's Day program. Coretta shared the Kings' experiences during the boycott and discussed the nonviolent protest movement begun by the SCLC. She also performed selections from the Freedom Concert program that she had premiered two years earlier in New York City.

On her return the Kings decided to take a vacation—their first since their marriage. They spent two weeks in Mexico, but "the contrast between the luxurious living of the rich and the wretched condition of the poor made Martin alternately rage and despair," Coretta recalled.

On September 17 Martin's first book, *Stride Toward Freedom,* was published, and Martin flew to New York for a

During a book signing in New York City's Harlem neighborhood, Martin was stabbed by a mentally unstable black woman. Here, Coretta sits with her husband in the Harlem hospital where he recuperated from the attack.

book signing while Coretta stayed home with the children. Two days later she was expecting Martin to arrive home. Instead, she received a phone call telling her that Martin had been stabbed during a book signing at a department store in Harlem. He had been rushed to Harlem Hospital for surgery. "He's alive," she was told, "but it is serious, very serious."

Coretta flew to New York, accompanied by Ralph Abernathy and Martin's sister, Christine. "All the hours I was en route, I kept thinking about the possibility of Martin's death," Coretta wrote years after the event. "At the same time I tried to tell myself that he would survive."

It turned out that Martin had been very lucky. He had been stabbed with a very sharp letter opener, the blade of which had come to rest against his aorta. If he had made a sudden movement or even sneezed, he would have died instantly. Looking at her barely conscious husband, Coretta silently came to terms with the fact that Martin could be killed at any time. His work in the protest movement had made him a marked man. Ironically, although the threat was most worrisome in the South, where many whites seethed with resentment over his attempts to bring about racial justice, this near-fatal attack had come in Harlem, and the assailant, Mrs. Isola Curry, was a mentally unstable black woman.

The attack on her husband seemed to strengthen Coretta's faith rather than weaken it. She did feel that it was a portent, though. She wrote in her autobiography,

> I thanked God for what seemed almost a miracle. . . . I knew that it was God's grace that had kept [Martin] alive and that He would sustain us during this period. Although there was much anxiety and concern for his life by his family, friends, and millions of followers over the world, Martin was calm—and so was I. It was as if both of us knew that this was not the time—that this trial was preparing us for something that was still to come.

By December Martin had fully recovered. This was one Christmas that Coretta was especially grateful to see.

Early the next year, the Kings traveled to India. While Martin explored the homeland of his spiritual mentor, Gandhi,

Coretta was busy performing Freedom Concerts throughout India to educate that country's people about the black struggle for social justice in America.

Coretta and Martin returned to Montgomery with renewed dedication to the principles of nonviolence and a new commitment to the SCLC's voter registration drive. So that Martin could be closer to the organization's main headquarters, the Kings decided to move to Atlanta. Martin handed the presidency of the MIA over to Ralph Abernathy and was named his father's co-pastor at the Ebenezer Baptist Church in February 1960. The family rented a modest house a few blocks away from the church.

As soon as the Kings were settled, Coretta joined the local branch of the Women's International League for Peace and Freedom, which worked to stop nuclear proliferation by convincing world leaders to outlaw the testing of atomic weapons. Coretta was proud to join the group. She knew that any contribution she made to the world's peace movement would also aid the black civil rights struggle by helping to unite all people.

She also found her family's mettle tested yet again. Not long after settling in Atlanta, Martin was indicted by the state of Alabama for allegedly falsifying his income tax returns for 1956 and 1957—which implied that he had pocketed income from the MIA and the SCLC. Coretta felt that this attack on her husband's integrity was harder on him than anything he had ever endured.

The case went to trial in Montgomery. To Coretta's astonishment, on May 28, 1960, a jury of 12 white men acquitted Martin. She couldn't stay and celebrate with her husband, however: She was scheduled to speak at three separate church services in Cleveland the next day for Women's Day. Coretta went directly from the Montgomery courthouse to Cleveland, arriving at 5:00 A.M. Her first speech was scheduled for 11:00 that morning, and she hadn't had any time to prepare a presentation. Ralph Abernathy, who had accompanied her, said, "Coretta, I think you ought to speak about your experience this week; just talk about that."

She did just that—for 40 minutes. Speaking extemporaneously about "those long days in court, the terrible anxiety, and the triumphant conclusion," Coretta captured and held her audience's attention. Their enthusiastic response afterward confirmed that her husband was not the only member of the family who possessed a gift for oratory.

DADDY GOES TO JAIL

Around this time, black college students began to heed the call for nonviolent protests against social injustice. In April 1960 more than 350 students from colleges throughout the South met at Shaw University in Raleigh, North Carolina, to form a youth organization to coordinate mass protests. Black students had previously held a series of sit-ins at department store lunch counters to demand that black customers be served. During these sit-ins, students sat in silence and refused to move for white customers. The sit-in movement was spreading to cities in North Carolina, Virginia, and Florida, and it needed a national group to keep people's passions alive.

The Student Nonviolent Coordinating Committee (SNCC, pronounced *snick*) was born at Shaw University, and Martin Luther King, Jr., and Ella Baker agreed to serve as the group's advisors. The SCLC provided office space and funding for the students.

In October Martin and a group of 75 black students and civic leaders staged a sit-in at Rich's Department Store in Atlanta. More than 30 people, including Martin, were arrested and taken to Atlanta's Fulton County jail. Images of the protestors singing "We Shall Overcome" filled the television airwaves.

Five days later, the mayor released all the sit-in protesters except Martin. He was taken to a jail in DeKalb County—the reputed headquarters of the Ku Klux Klan. Although cleared of charges relating to the sit-in, Martin was held on an old probation violation that stemmed from an invalid driver's license. The judge sentenced Martin to six months of hard labor at the state penitentiary in Reidsville, 300 miles away from Atlanta.

Coretta was five months pregnant with her third child, and the news came as a shock. Feeling alone and sorry for herself, she broke down and cried. It was the first—and only—time Coretta wept in public

The King children had heard the news of their father's arrest on the radio and tearfully asked their mother, "Why did Daddy go to jail?"

Coretta had been prepared for the question and replied, "Your daddy is a brave and kind man. He went to jail to help people." Coretta was gratified when, soon after, Yoki was taunted by a young white classmate for having a father in jail, and she put the girl in her place with a simple, "Yes, he goes to jail to help people."

Coretta worried about her husband, though. This was a man who "needed and depended upon the support of people he loved." It would be a long time away from that support.

One day, Coretta got an unexpected phone call from Senator John F. Kennedy, the Democratic candidate for president in the 1960 election. He told her he was concerned about Martin and his family and offered to help in any way he could. Coretta was most appreciative.

Senator Kennedy kept his word. His campaign manager and younger brother, Robert, called the judge in Martin's case. Before Coretta knew it, Martin had been released from prison on a $2,000 bond. The SCLC flew him home to Atlanta. Later that fall, Senator John F. Kennedy won the presidential election by a slim margin—a margin that Coretta always attributed to his intervention on Martin's behalf.

On January 30, 1961, Coretta gave birth to her third child, Dexter Scott King. Thanks to the Kennedys' intervention, Martin was free to share in this happy event.

7

Birmingham

The civil-rights movement kept picking up steam. In the spring of
1961, sit-ins progressed to Freedom Rides, which were aimed
at desegregating interstate bus lines and terminals. As the movement escalated, so did the violence. Hardcore racists seemed to
be particularly infuriated by the volunteer interracial Freedom
Riders—mostly idealistic college students—pairs of whom
rode buses throughout the South. Coretta recalled being
horrified by TV news reports of smashed and burning buses,
the riders beaten and thrown in jail.

The Freedom Riders would not back down, and Coretta
and Martin were impressed by the kids' determination.
Coretta felt that she and her husband had "gained a welcome
ally in southern college students who committed themselves
to nonviolent action." Throughout this period, Martin and
his fellow activists were repeatedly jailed for leading illegal
marches and holding sit-ins or any number of other by-the-book

charges. Coretta generally stayed away from the sit-ins and other protests. Having their mother jailed as well would be too much for her children to bear.

FIGHTING FOR WORLD PEACE

In March 1962 Coretta was asked to participate in a meeting to be held in Geneva, Switzerland. Women from Scandinavia, Britain, the U.S.S.R., and Australia as well as the United States would be meeting in an effort to establish an international ban on the testing of all atomic weapons. The trip was sponsored by Women Strike for Peace, a Quaker group, and Coretta would be one of a group of 50 American women, four of whom were black. With her husband so embroiled in the civil-rights movement, Coretta felt that it was up to her to pursue the ultimate goal of world peace.

On the plane to Geneva, Coretta felt very much at home in the company of so many bright and politically active women. She had high hopes, therefore, for the success of the conference.

The trip proved disappointing. Arthur Dean, the American representative at the conference, brushed off the American women's delegation. Coretta later wrote that she felt that Dean had perceived the delegation as a group of "hysterical" women

IN HER OWN WORDS...

The cause of world peace is one in which Coretta has been actively involved since her college days. At Antioch she worked with Quaker groups and then became a member of the Women's International League for Peace and Freedom when she moved to Atlanta. She firmly believes that it is up to women to achieve this ultimate goal. As she wrote in her autobiography:

> I was, and still am, convinced that the women of the world, united without any regard for national or racial divisions, can become a most powerful force for international peace and brotherhood.

rather than as a serious organization of concerned citizens. The meeting ended abruptly when Dean advised the women to consult the Soviet government.

The women did just that—and received a much more welcoming reaction. The Soviets openly discussed nuclear testing with them and even held a reception to honor them. Although impressed by the cordial treatment the women received from the Soviets, Coretta realized that "the Russians were masters of the art of propaganda" and would as a matter of course treat them well to elicit a positive response. Once back on the plane to the United States, Coretta couldn't help but wonder why the Americans had resisted the delegation's efforts to discuss the issue of nuclear testing. The nonviolent protest movement struggled against the inequities of racism, but Coretta also saw sexism as an undeniable and stifling injustice.

THE STRUGGLE CONTINUES

The SCLC's voter registration campaign was relaunched in Albany, Georgia, in the summer of 1961. In the blink of an eye, the campaign blossomed into a sit-in protest against segregation in Albany—one that continued for a year. Martin and Ralph Abernathy—who by now also had moved his family to Atlanta—traveled to Albany to help negotiate with city officials and police. The two leaders were jailed repeatedly but were always released before their plight could arouse public sympathy. Although President Kennedy was contacted several times to see whether the federal government would intervene in the negotiations, the White House never responded. The silence of the Kennedy administration during the yearlong crisis was also unsettling.

The nonviolent movement was seven years old. Coretta now realized that racism, embedded as it was in the hearts and minds of many Americans, would be far more difficult to overcome than she had ever imagined. Just as Coretta and her women colleagues had not been taken seriously by the

The SCLC's antisegregation campaign in Albany would last for a full year. During that time, Martin was arrested repeatedly by Albany police, including at the time this picture was taken, July 27, 1962.

U.S. government in Geneva, it seemed that the entire non-violent civil-rights movement was being dismissed not only by southern authorities, but also by the federal government.

The Kings would not give up. They continued the struggle and grew wiser in the process.

GROWING UP AS A KING

Raising children in the segregated South was hard enough. Raising the children of Martin Luther King, Jr., was even harder. Coretta felt that the kids often bore the burden—both good and bad—of having such a famous man as their father. She strived to "strike a balance" for them. She recalled in her autobiography a time when Yoki, then seven, demonstrated "a unique ability to handle her own problems." After being repeatedly singled out by her classmates for being the daughter of Martin Luther King, Jr., and all that that entailed, the girl took matters into her own hands: "One day she came home from school with a look of satisfaction on her face. She told me that she had just 'got tired of the whole thing' and . . . when her teacher stepped out of the classroom, Yoki had turned to the other children and said, 'Look, all I want is just to be treated like a normal child.'" Coretta was both amused and proud, for Yoki "had articulated, in her childish wisdom, exactly what Martin and I had in mind for our children."

Marty had an even bigger challenge, because he carried his father's name in addition to the family connection. The name alone often induced hostility in whites. (He once confessed to Coretta that he had told two threatening white boys that he didn't know his father's name because he was afraid he'd be beaten up if he'd told them.) Plus, of course, the name had a built-in identity that wasn't necessarily his own.

Four-year-old Dexter had his own take on an ongoing effrontery. Coretta wrote of an occasion when her older children were telling her that they had been called "nigger" at the YWCA. While she struggled to help them cope, Dexter piped up and said, "Mommy, you know why some people say 'nigger'? [B]ecause they don't know *how* to say 'Negro.'"

Other injustices and humiliations were harder to deal with—such as why the kids couldn't enjoy a playground in a white neighborhood or why they couldn't go to the new Funtown amusement park that was being advertised endlessly. To spare the little ones more hurt to know that they weren't welcome at these places, Coretta and Martin came up with excuses, such as that they had to get home for lunch or they had to go on a trip.

Eventually the children learned the truth, but it wasn't too long after that Funtown was desegregated, and the King family enjoyed a delightful day there. Equally gratifying was the reaction Coretta got from one white woman at the park. After determining that Coretta was indeed Mrs. King, the woman told her, "Oh, I'm so glad you are here." She repeated the sentence to Yoki, then walked away.

Coretta recalled, "I kept thinking how wonderful it was that the children had been able to see that what their daddy was doing had brought concrete results in their own lives."

THE BATTLE FOR BIRMINGHAM

A meeting with President John F. Kennedy and Attorney General Robert F. Kennedy was at the top of the SCLC's agenda for 1963. In January Martin met with the Kennedys to discuss the need for a new civil rights bill because the Civil Rights Act of 1957 had not proved very effective, and blacks throughout the South continued to suffer. President Kennedy listened sympathetically but offered no help. He explained that if he were to introduce any civil-rights legislation, other important legislation that he was about to propose to the Congress would be jeopardized.

Frustrated by the lack of government support, the SCLC went forward with a plan to desegregate a city known as a bedrock of white supremacy: Birmingham, Alabama. The city's entrenched hatred of blacks was legendary. Throughout the late 1950s and early 1960s, Birmingham witnessed more than 50 cross burnings, along with 15 racially motivated bombings. Eugene "Bull" Connor, the city's commissioner of public safety, used the police to terrorize blacks, and Alabama governor George Wallace proudly proclaimed that he would do everything in his power to keep the races separate and unequal, so blacks in Birmingham could not appeal to the state government for help.

The SCLC began organizing in Birmingham early in the year. Coretta was expecting the Kings' fourth child and was approaching her due date. As Coretta explained to *Essence*

Coretta is shown here playing with her youngest child, Bernice. Because Martin was planning to lead a march in Birmingham in April, Coretta took castor oil to induce an early labor. Bernice was born on March 28, 1963.

magazine in 1999, she and Martin resorted to drastic action "to time her delivery . . . because Martin was planning to lead a march in Birmingham, and he wanted his inevitable arrest there to happen on April 12, Good Friday, for its symbolism. So I took castor oil to induce an early labor, and Bernice was born on March 28, while Martin was still in town." Coretta didn't have her husband around for long. Martin was off to Birmingham the next day.

On April 3 Martin declared the start of a mass protest movement to desegregate all of the city's public facilities and transportation systems and to urge local retail stores to hire black employees. African Americans both young and old heeded the call to join the sit-ins and marches. Protests took place at lunch counters and in front of department stores. During the first few days, more than 300 people were arrested.

The city eventually got an injunction from the state court to forbid protest demonstrations, but the SCLC wouldn't back down. They decided to violate the injunction with a march to city hall on Good Friday. Just as they had anticipated, both Martin and Ralph Abernathy were arrested and held in solitary confinement in the Birmingham jail.

Coretta and the children waited in Atlanta for word from Martin. He was jailed so often that phone calls from prison had become routine. This time no phone call came, and Coretta knew something was wrong. Lawyers were barred from seeing the two men, who weren't allowed to communicate with anyone.

By Easter Sunday, still with no word, Coretta took matters into her own hands: She called the White House. The president was not available, but Attorney General Robert Kennedy returned Coretta's call, explaining that his brother was tending to their very ill father, but how could he help? She explained the situation and asked if the president could find out about her husband's condition.

Robert Kennedy was well aware of Bull Connor's reputation. Finding out about Martin and Abernathy would not be easy. But he promised to inquire. The next day President Kennedy himself called Coretta. He had spoken to city and police officials in Birmingham and was confident that her husband would be calling shortly.

To Coretta's great relief, Martin called home 15 minutes later. He was weary but unharmed. After learning from Coretta why he was suddenly being treated decently, he instructed her to have the SCLC leak the story of the president's involvement to the press. The plan worked. After the nation learned of what had happened, people paid a lot more attention to Birmingham and to the nonviolent movement.

THE CHILDREN'S CRUSADE

To sustain public interest in the protest, the SCLC leaders

decided to recruit high school and college students, hoping that their youth and innocence would drum up popular support for the battle against Birmingham's racists. Recruiters set out for every high school and black college in Birmingham, and the kids "responded by the thousands," Coretta wrote in her autobiography. After receiving training in the art of non-violence, their protest began.

On May 2, more than 1,000 youth marched from Birmingham's Sixteenth Street Baptist Church into town; 959 of them were arrested. The next day more kids joined the march. This time Bull Connor ordered his men to blast the youngsters with high-pressure fire hoses and unleash the police dogs. Soon the marchers were soaked with water, bleeding from dog bites, and battered by police clubs. Outraged black onlookers started throwing rocks at the police.

The Children's Crusade continued for another week. By now the city's jails were overflowing, and the police broke up demonstrations but didn't arrest anyone because there was no place to incarcerate them. The march had had its effect: Thousands of telegrams were being sent to the White House by citizens horrified and disgusted by what they were seeing on their televisions.

Equally appalled, President Kennedy dispatched a negotiator to Birmingham on May 4, to mediate between the SCLC and white business and civic leaders. The president's intervention did the trick. A week later city officials agreed to desegregate public places such as stores and parks. Retailers also agreed to integrate their lunch counters and hire black employees. Furthermore, black and white leaders were to meet regularly to continue resolving their differences.

"Of course, that was not the end of it," Coretta later wrote. Some of the fresh chaos touched the King family personally. Martin's brother, A.D. King, who lived in Birmingham, had his home firebombed, and the motel where Martin had been staying while protesting was also bombed. Rioting broke out after the bombings. People were fed up with the cowardly terrorist tactics of Birmingham's white hate groups.

Despite the destruction and turmoil, the SCLC could claim real victory against the evil of segregation. Events in Birmingham had forced the federal government to reexamine its position, and, on June 11, 1963, President Kennedy held a press conference and announced his intention to support a civil-rights bill that would outlaw racial segregation in all public facilities. The bill would give the government the right to sue businesses and organizations that refused to integrate. It would also reinforce the Supreme Court's decision in *Brown* v. *Board of Education* and pressure states to fully integrate their public schools.

Not long after, Coretta recalled, President Kennedy told Dr. King with amusement, "Bull Connor has done as much for civil rights as Abraham Lincoln."

THE MARCH ON WASHINGTON

On August 28, 1963, the spark that had ignited in Birmingham burned brightly in the nation's capital. Nearly 250,000 people—black, white, Native American, Latino, Asian, young, old, rich, and poor—marched from the Washington Monument to the steps of the Lincoln Memorial. The March on Washington for Jobs and Freedom was a mass call for justice for all American people regardless of race, sex, creed, or economic status. It was the largest peaceful mass demonstration in the history of the United States—and Martin Luther King, Jr., had been allotted eight minutes to speak.

Sitting behind her husband on the speaker's platform, looking out at the sea of faces dripping with sweat in the intense heat, Coretta beamed with pride as Martin began his speech. Listening to his oration, she sensed that he had abandoned his prepared speech and that his words were inspired by God.

Martin acknowledges the crowd in Washington, D.C., at the site of his famous "I Have a Dream" speech. Listening to her husband speak, Coretta said it felt like "Heaven itself had opened up."

Of all the speeches and sermons he had given, this one, Coretta knew, would be the most meaningful of his life. His words were simple and profound:

> I have a dream that my four little children one day will live in a nation where they will not be judged by the color of their skin, but by the content of their character. I have a dream today!

Coretta felt that everyone listening was being transformed, that "Heaven itself opened up." The speech was drawing to a close:

> When we allow freedom to ring from every state and every city, we will be able to speed up that day when all of God's children, black men and white men, Jews and Gentiles, Protestants and Catholics, will be able to join hands and sing in the words of the old Negro spiritual, "Free at last! Free at last! Great God A-mighty, we are free at last!"

8

"What Are You Afraid Of?"

"Tragedy came snapping on the heels of triumph," Coretta wrote in *My Life with Martin Luther King, Jr.* On September 15, 1963, just weeks after Martin's triumphant speech in Washington, D.C., the Sixteenth Street Baptist Church in Birmingham was bombed. Four young girls were killed. This awful event followed the June assassination of the Kings' close friend Medgar Evers, head of the NAACP in Mississippi. Even as Coretta and Martin were enjoying hard-won triumphs, such horrific incidents were terrible reminders of how much work was still to be done.

Then on November 22, 1963, an event that shattered the entire nation occurred.

Coretta and Martin were both at home. Coretta was talking to a friend on the telephone when Martin yelled from upstairs that a news report said that President Kennedy had been shot, perhaps even killed. She hung up the phone and rushed upstairs. The Kings watched the news in silence. Then the update they were dreading came: The president was dead.

Martin and Coretta looked at each other in disbelief. The loss of President Kennedy was a devastating blow, both personally and politically. The president had been an ally in the nonviolent movement and a supporter of the SCLC's goals in troubled times. Martin finally spoke. "This is what is going to happen to me also."

Coretta stared at her husband, unable to reassure him. There was nothing she could say. Because, in fact, she felt that he was right. She held Martin's hand tightly.

Soon their children came rushing home from school, and Coretta tried to comfort them. Yoki, especially, was distraught. She feared that, with Kennedy dead, their chance for freedom had died with him. Coretta gathered her daughter into her arms and told her, "God is still above, and He's going to take care of us. So don't you worry, we're going to get our freedom."

OH, FREEDOM

John Kennedy had been killed just as he was trying to pass civil-rights legislation through Congress. To the surprise of many, on July 2, 1964, the country's new president, Lyndon B. Johnson, signed his predecessor's civil-rights bill into law. Martin was one of several black civic and religious leaders invited to the White House to witness the event. His first meeting with Johnson helped reassure him that the new president, a son of the South, was on the side of civil rights.

Coretta and Martin kept up their fight for voting rights for blacks, with stunning success. In just two years, 1963 and 1964, 70,000 black voters were added to the rolls in Georgia alone.

A LIFE REWARDED

Throughout the summer and early fall of 1964, both Coretta and Martin did a great deal of traveling. While Martin flew to

Germany and to the Vatican for a private audience with Pope Paul VI, Coretta was busy giving Freedom Concerts. She was not too busy to worry about Martin's health, however. In October she convinced him to go to an Atlanta hospital for a complete checkup.

One morning soon after Martin had been admitted, Coretta received a call from a reporter who had exciting news: The Reverend Dr. Martin Luther King, Jr., had won the Nobel Peace Prize for 1964. Coretta was almost dumbstruck. She knew that her husband was being considered for the prize but for him to actually win what is arguably the most prestigious honor in the world had seemed extremely unlikely. Coretta immediately called Martin at the hospital. "How is the Nobel Peace Prize winner for 1964 feeling this morning?" she recalled asking her husband.

A few days later Martin left the hospital with a clean bill of health, and the King family joyously made preparations for the trip to Norway for the award ceremony. A group of local ministers paid for plane tickets for Martin's parents. (Although the children were anxious to go, no one under age 12 was allowed at the ceremony.)

A month before attending the Nobel ceremony in Norway, Coretta flew to New York to begin another series of Freedom Concerts to raise money for the SCLC. She performed an eight-part composition, called *The Story of the Struggle from 1955 to 1965*, on November 14 at New York City's Town Hall. The concert raised $6,000 for the movement. Then she performed a second concert, this one in New Jersey.

Finally early in December Coretta, Martin, and about 30 other people flew to New York; Martin was to be honored by the United Nations for his Nobel win. From New York they headed to London, where Martin gave a sermon in St. Paul's Cathedral. Coretta noted in her autobiography, "Except for the Nobel ceremony itself, this was the high moment of the trip." She found herself "tremendously moved" by the Anglican ritual—and, of course, by her husband's sermon. The sermon held a special significance for Coretta "because it was the theme of the first [one] I had ever heard him preach . . . in a little church in Roxbury, Massachusetts."

On December 8 the group—which included the Abernathys and Andrew Young—flew to Oslo, where Martin and Coretta were greeted not only by officials from the Nobel Committee but also by a huge crowd of well-wishers. The warmth of the crowd was unexpected for Coretta and made her feel "very much at home." Two days later, in a ceremony at Oslo University, King Olav V of Norway presented Dr. Martin Luther King, Jr., with the Nobel Peace Prize: a gold medal, a scroll, and a cash prize. Coretta considered it an emotional high point of their life together.

A BATTLE IS WON . . .

Not long after the Kings returned home in triumph, voter registration campaigns in Selma, Alabama, and nearby Marion got dangerous and bloody. On February 1, Martin and Ralph Abernathy were arrested and jailed in Selma.

Coretta and Juanita Abernathy went to Selma during their husbands' five-day imprisonment. Soon after their arrival, Coretta learned that former Black Muslim leader Malcolm X was at that moment speaking in the local A.M.E. church, where the spellbinding orator had roused the beleaguered demonstrators with his message condoning retaliatory violence. Coretta entered the church and took a turn addressing the crowd—and, in contrast to Malcolm X, she stressed the importance of nonviolence.

Afterward when she got the chance to meet Malcolm, Coretta found him apologetic about any difficulty his presence might have caused that day. He had intended quite the opposite, in fact. Coretta wrote in her autobiography that Malcolm told her he had come to Selma to make it easier for Martin: "If the white people realize what the alternative is, perhaps they will be more willing to hear Dr. King." He also expressed regret that he wouldn't be able to visit Martin in jail as he had hoped because he had to fly to London. (It turned out that the British authorities wouldn't let Malcolm in their country, so he returned to America—and was assassinated in Harlem just a couple of weeks later, on February 21, 1965. The assassination of Malcolm X so soon after their meeting left Coretta both saddened and ambivalent toward some of the slain leader's beliefs. Indeed, although for years he had preached attaining black liberation "by any means necessary" and argued for separation of the races, toward the end of his life he had been taking a more moderate stance.)

... BUT THE COST IS HIGH

One of the Selma protest marches led to the death of a young black man whose aunt had been a childhood friend of Coretta's. On February 26, 1965, Jimmie Lee Jackson died of a gunshot wound he had sustained eight days earlier while trying to protect his mother from an attack by a state trooper.

Matters came to a head when the police, under the command of Selma's sheriff, Jim Clark, attacked more than 150 black students who were demonstrating peacefully outside a city courthouse. Clark's men forced the students to jog to a jail six miles outside of town, repeatedly shocking them with electric cattle prods to hurry them along. In response to these sickening events, the SCLC sponsored a march from Selma to Montgomery—a distance of more than 50 miles—to force Governor Wallace to rein in police and to demand justice at the ballot box.

The march took place on Sunday, March 7, 1965, but as more than 500 mostly black marchers reached the Edmund Pettus Bridge on their way to Montgomery, they were met by a barricade of dozens of Alabama state troopers and mounted cavalry. Ordered to turn back, the marchers refused, giving the police the excuse they needed to launch an all-out attack using tear gas grenades, cattle prods, clubs, and bullwhips from their charging horses.

Coretta got word of this "Bloody Sunday" just before giving a Freedom Concert in San Francisco as part of a six-city West Coast tour. Martin called her to tell her of his plan to personally lead another march that Tuesday, with Ralph Abernathy at his side.

The significant difference of this march and the tragic attempt made two days earlier was that roughly half of the 1,500 marchers were white. One striking similarity remained: the blockade of troopers and horsemen at the Edmund Pettus Bridge. Fearing more bloodshed, King ordered the marchers to turn back.

President Johnson had been watching the developments in Selma. Overriding Governor Wallace, Johnson had the federal government take control of the Alabama National Guard and assigned them to protect the civil-rights marchers.

On March 21, the SCLC leadership and thousands of supporters left Selma for Montgomery on a four-day march. Coretta had a speaking engagement at Bennett College in North Carolina that day, but she joined Martin on the second day of the march. The marchers sang gospel songs and chanted, "We want freedom!" on a trek that was punctuated by rain and mud. Finally they reached Montgomery and the steps of the capitol.

On August 6, 1965, President Johnson signed the Voting Rights Act. Coupled with the Civil Rights Act of 1964, the Voting Rights Act signaled the demise of the southern system of racial discrimination that had existed since slavery.

INTEGRATION ON THE HOME FRONT

That summer, the Atlanta public schools were finally integrated. Coretta suddenly realized that she would have to act quickly to enroll Yoki and Marty in one of the previously all-white elementary schools for them to start in September.

The King children did not want to be the only two black kids in school, so Coretta convinced Juanita Abernathy to register her three children, as well. The women agreed on the Spring Street School, which had a reputation as one of Atlanta's finest.

They took their children to the school for registration, and the school's principal made them feel welcome. When a reporter approached, however, the principal made it clear that she did not want any publicity about the event. Coretta disagreed. "I felt that it was extremely important that the nation see that integration could be accomplished peacefully," she wrote, hoping, too, that their experience would encourage other black families to do the same. Thus, when a reporter appeared at her house later that morning, she didn't hesitate to give him all the details. This was one time when Coretta wanted the entire nation to see her children walking in their father's footsteps.

A NEW STRUGGLE

With the passage of the Civil Rights Act and the Voting Rights Act, the civil-rights movement had accomplished what it had set out to do. The Kings felt it was now time to take their activism in a different direction—literally. In January 1966 they decided to move into a public housing unit in Chicago, where they would launch the Poor People's Campaign. This, they hoped, would shine the spotlight on the plight of poor urban blacks. In larger cities throughout the North, many blacks lived in ghettos that separated them from mainstream American life, consigning them to live either in crumbling tenements or cramped housing projects neglected by city landlords. The rate of unemployment among northern urban blacks was high compared to other racial groups, as well. As in the South, education at predominantly black public schools was usually inferior to that offered by schools in all-white neighborhoods, and school

When the Atlanta public schools were finally integrated, Coretta acted quickly to enroll Yoki and Marty in one of the previously all-white elementary schools. Here, she sings with her four children at home after church.

buildings in ghetto areas were frequently decrepit and poorly equipped.

Life in a housing project was a jarring adjustment for Coretta and her family. She noted with grim amusement that the landlord had haphazardly painted the apartment in anticipation of his famous tenants, but the hallways still reeked of urine, the plumbing and heating were still substandard, and "there was nothing green in sight" as far as playgrounds for children were concerned.

In July 1966 the Kings—including the children—led a crowd of 50,000 on a mile-long march to Chicago's city hall, where Martin nailed a list of demands for Mayor Richard Daley onto the door. This symbolic gesture recalled his namesake Martin Luther's nailing of the 95 Theses to a door at Germany's University of Wittenberg in 1517. King's list outlined demands for fairness in public housing and integration of white neighborhoods.

The next morning, however, Mayor Daley dismissed the demands out of hand. As news of this decision spread, discouragement hung in the oppressive summer air in the ghetto. Then the police began shutting off fire hydrants that some neighborhood kids had turned on to cool themselves—a

IN HER OWN WORDS...

Sending her own children to a newly integrated school was very important to Coretta because she firmly believed in being a role model. Although she wished that integration would be a two-way street, she harbored no illusions about that prospect. As she wrote in her autobiography:

Although we believe that the process should work both ways—white families sharing the burden of "pioneering" with black students by going to all-black schools—we knew that that was not a likely prospect anywhere in this country, and especially not in the South.

common practice in ghettos. In retaliation, the kids started throwing rocks at the police and breaking windows. Soon local gangs got involved, shooting started, and the violence escalated. The situation developed into a full-scale riot.

Scattered rioting stretched into the next day, during which Coretta spoke at a women's meeting at the local YWCA. "I was supposed to talk about unity, but that was hardly the day for it," she recalled in her autobiography. The neighborhood women shared her mood. When it was suggested that they send a telegram to Mayor Daley urging him to support the SCLC's list of fair housing demands, many of the women were reluctant to sign it. Coretta guessed that perhaps their husbands held city jobs, and the women feared that they could be fired.

"What are you afraid of?" Coretta finally asked. "There comes a time when we have to make a decision and we have to make a choice." The women responded by not only signing the telegram but also by forming an integrated organization, called Women Mobilized for Change, dedicated to improving local living conditions.

When the rioting finally ended, two black people—one of them a 14-year-old girl—were dead. The SCLC decided to make integrating Chicago's housing its top priority. Marches into all-white working-class neighborhoods were scheduled. Martin personally led a march into Marquette Park on August 5, 1966. That day 600 people—including many whites—followed him through Chicago's white communities. The residents' responses were horrifying. People threw rocks and bottles at the marchers, shouting "Nigger!", "Coon!", and "Go back to Africa!" Martin later told Coretta that he had never experienced such intense hatred—not even in the South.

The rioting spurred Coretta to return to Atlanta with their children, although her husband continued to spend half of each week in Chicago. Finally, on August 26, the city agreed to open housing, which the SCLC had been striving for most.

Then the SCLC began Operation Breadbasket, aimed at putting more money back into the ghetto there, in Chicago. It was led by a young minister named Jesse Jackson.

BLACK VERSUS BLACK

Coretta had been actively involved in the world-peace movement since her college days. In 1967 her fervent dedication to peace convinced her husband to denounce America's involvement in the Vietnam War. The Kings believed that, aside from it being morally wrong for the United States to be involved in another country's civil war and costing thousands of young—and mostly poor black—American soldiers their lives and limbs, the cost of military defense was draining the country's resources for social programs. In a speech Martin gave on April 4, 1967, he noted that the government spent an estimated "$322,000 for each enemy we kill" yet only "$53 for each person classified as poor."

Although Coretta was glad to see Martin embracing a worldwide push for peace as part of his nonviolent philosophy, many black civil rights leaders criticized him for shifting his attention away from the black struggle for equality. Also, some blacks agreed with the government's position on Vietnam, so he risked alienating them from the civil-rights movement.

Coretta considered the criticism to her husband's stance a double-standard, noting, "I . . . pointed out that Pope Paul had recently . . . spoken against the war, and my husband was really saying the same things. When the Pope spoke, everyone applauded; but when a black man named Martin Luther King speaks, they criticize him." Coretta had been looking forward to taking part in a peace demonstration in New York with her husband. Instead—and to her disappointment—he booked her to give a speech in San Francisco on that same day.

Criticism of the Kings was becoming fairly commonplace, especially among young blacks, who felt that their nonviolent approach to civil protest was too slow and ineffective. Up and coming young black leaders—like Huey P. Newton, founder of the Black Panther Party, and Stokely Carmichael, who began his involvement in the civil rights movement with SNCC and then migrated to the Black Panther Party—felt that the recently passed civil-rights laws were "too little too late." Groups such as the Black Panthers and the Nation of Islam preached the militant idea of Black Power—forcing society to change through violence—over the faith-based protests that the Kings had always advocated. In 1965 the riot in the Los Angeles section of Watts that protested the brutal beating of a black man set the stage. By 1967 rebellions by urban blacks had erupted in more than 100 U.S. cities.

AN ERA ENDS

Martin's answer to this dissatisfaction was the Poor People's Campaign—an initiative to organize the nation's poor, regardless of race, from ten cities and five rural towns in a mass protest to demand "economic security, decent sanitary housing, and quality education" for every American. The protesters would build a tent city in the heart of Washington, D.C., to demonstrate

IN HER OWN WORDS...

Coretta was a staunch supporter of world peace and believed that supporting world peace—especially as it regarded the war in Vietnam—was an inevitable partner of the civil rights movement. As she wrote in her autobiography, *My Life with Martin Luther King, Jr.*:

> I believed that to combine the spiritual essence of the peace movement and the civil-rights movement would bring a lot of good people in this country together. The peace movement was composed primarily of whites who would be brought into closer cooperation with us. It would become one movement for good. You cannot separate peace and freedom: They are inextricably related.

their plight. The nonviolent movement was slowly shifting its focus from a civil-rights struggle to a human-rights struggle.

Then in February 1968 the sanitation workers union in Memphis, Tennessee, went on strike to protest unfair treatment by the mayor. The predominantly black union had tried for several weeks to launch a mass march, but the city's police were blocking their every move. A union leader and SCLC contact in Memphis called Dr. King and asked him to help the garbage collectors mount a protest. He agreed.

The event was a disaster. Martin arrived in Memphis to discover the march already in progress—and terribly undisciplined, with some of the marchers advocating violence. Violence abruptly ended the protest, as well. One man was shot during the frenzy.

Deeply troubled, Martin returned to Atlanta. It was the first time extreme disorder had occurred during a march under his leadership. He wanted to go back to Memphis as soon as possible to prove that nonviolent tactics could work.

A heated debate ensued among the other SCLC leaders, many of whom were eager to move on and felt that Martin should direct his energies toward their Poor People's Campaign. Martin, however, was determined to make things right in Memphis.

On Wednesday, April 3, Coretta awoke before dawn to cook breakfast for Martin and Ralph Abernathy before their return trip to Memphis. When Coretta later recalled kissing her husband good-bye, she described it as a farewell "like thousands of other times before." The two men dashed to Abernathy's car, and Coretta watched them drive down the street as the sun peeked over the horizon. She would never see Martin alive again.

In Memphis that evening, Dr. King stood in front of a crowd of 2,000 supporters outside a church and told them that he would lead a march on April 8, despite a federal injunction that the city had secured to stop the protest. He said that the

Dr. Martin Luther King, Jr., makes his final public appearance in Memphis, Tennessee. There, he announced that despite a federal injunction, he would lead a march of local garbage collectors and others on April 8.

march was more than a demonstration for local garbage collectors: It was a public testament to the moral justice of nonviolence and proof that no evil could match the Christian belief in the power of love.

"Then," Coretta wrote in *My Life with Martin Luther King, Jr.*, "the mantle of prophecy seemed to descend upon Martin." Against the eerie backdrop of a spring storm that was brewing outside, Martin told the demonstrators, "Like anybody else, I would like to live a long life. Longevity has its place. But I'm not concerned with that now. I just want to do God's will."

So it was that the next day, April 4, Martin Luther King, Jr., was standing on his motel balcony, briefly alone, preparing to join his friends and associates for a quick dinner before attending a meeting. In that instant he was fatally shot. In that instant came the end of an era in the history of civil rights.

9

Black Madonna

Immediately after Martin Luther King, Jr.'s, assassination, rioting erupted all across the United States. Even in those first bleak days after her husband's death, Coretta Scott King knew, however, that his dream of justice and peace could not be allowed to die with him.

Countless newspaper stories covered her husband's funeral. Reporters compared Coretta's demeanor with the dignified air of former first lady Jacqueline Kennedy at President Kennedy's funeral in 1963. Words such as *grace, resilience, courage,* and *strength* were used frequently. One reporter, after observing her during the funeral service at Ebenezer Baptist Church, described Coretta as a "Black Madonna"—likening her to African-American depictions of Mary.

This flood of praise may have come as a surprise to Coretta, who later wrote admiringly of Mrs. Kennedy's deportment during the president's funeral. Despite her quiet courage,

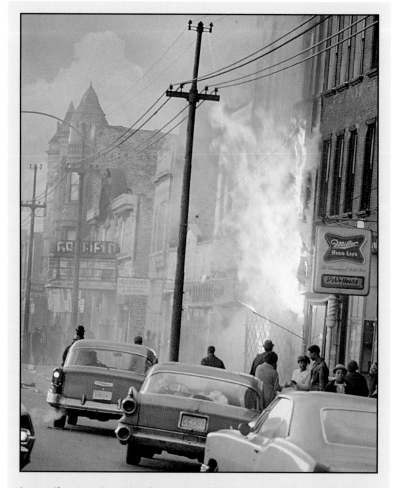

Immediately after Martin's assassination, rioting erupted all across the United States. Here, one of the many fires set by looters rages out of control in Chicago.

Coretta felt vulnerable even as she consoled her children and attended to Martin's unfinished business affairs. Coretta's religious faith and the love and concern of friends from near and far were her only anchors.

Harry Belafonte provided a shoulder for Coretta to lean on. He also had provided for her and her children's financial security: Martin had not made elaborate plans for his family's financial security in the event of his death. In fact, he had been so unconcerned about wealth or possessions that he had given most of his earnings to the nonviolent movement and reportedly set aside just $5,000 for his family. Knowing this, according to *Ebony* magazine, Belafonte had taken out a $500,000 insurance policy in Martin's name years before the civil-rights leader's death.

KEEPER OF THE DREAM

Coretta almost instantly stepped into her husband's empty shoes to continue promoting his causes. Much of Martin's immediate work had to be completed, she believed, and this was not the time to become consumed by grief. She honored as many of her husband's public appearances and speaking engagements as possible. An antiwar rally in Central Park was planned for April 27, which happened to be Coretta's birthday. She searched through Martin's personal papers and found notes for a speech called "The 10 Commandments on Vietnam," which he had been preparing for the rally. Coretta used Martin's notes to make her presentation.

The Poor People's Campaign could not be canceled. On May 2, 1968, Coretta helped launch the campaign from the balcony of the Lorraine Motel in Memphis—the place where her husband had been struck down. Martin's brother stood with her as she unveiled a plaque to honor her late husband. Looking out at the audience of a thousand people, Coretta spoke earnestly: "I pledge eternal loyalty to the work my husband nobly began. His legacy will lead us to the point where all God's children have shoes."

The day before Dr. King's funeral, Coretta led the Memphis protest march that Martin had planed to lead. Her children beside her, she led a crowd of more than 25,000 marchers for a mile past the silent onlookers.

Several weeks later Coretta walked arm in arm with Ralph Abernathy, now president of the SCLC, during the largest rally of the Poor People's Campaign, the Solidarity Day march on June 19. Fifty thousand citizens—a rainbow of faces—came to show their support of Martin's dream of an integrated society. Coretta, attired in a black dress, low-heeled black shoes, and sunglasses, wore a white lily over her heart. She delivered the speech for her husband's last scheduled public appearance on the steps of the Lincoln Memorial.

"The problem[s] of racism, poverty, and war can all be summarized with one word: violence," Coretta declared. Yolanda, Martin III, Dexter, and little Bernice watched their mother from the stage platform, surrounded by SCLC members and family. As Coretta spoke, her years as a peace activist were evident. She spoke not only as the widow of Dr. Martin Luther King, Jr., but also as a woman and a mother. "Women, if the soul of this nation is to be saved, I believe that you must become its soul. You must speak out against the evils of our time as you see them," Coretta said. She urged women of all races to build a "solid block of women's power" for peace and equality in the world.

Her speech broke new ground. Few women, regardless of race, had ever had the opportunity to address the social, political, and economic ills of the nation in front of such a large gathering. Not only was she able to further her late husband's agenda for social change, but she also sent a rallying cry to American women by entreating them to join the front lines of the nonviolent struggle for human rights. Once again, Coretta's determination impressed reporters. The *New York Times* called her "a woman champion of equality for all races."

NEW DIRECTIONS

Winning personal adulation wasn't Coretta's goal. Continuing her husband's legacy was. That July she held a press conference in Atlanta to announce her plans to build the Martin Luther King, Jr., Center for Nonviolent Social Change. The King Center would be located in what would be known as the

Freedom Hall complex, which would include her husband's restored birthplace, his gravesite, the Ebenezer Baptist Church, a library and archive of his personal writings, a memorial park, a museum, and an institute dedicated to nonviolent social change and African-American studies. Coretta also told the nation about her fund-raising campaign to cover the costs of building the King Center. To collect donations for the project, Coretta vowed to travel throughout the United States and the world to spread her late husband's message of love and hope to people everywhere.

She then signed a contract with a major New York publisher, worth $50,000 according to press reports, to write the story of her life with Martin and their struggle for civil rights. To meet her deadline, she spent the rest of the summer alone in New England writing the book.

On January 15, 1969, Coretta celebrated what would have been Martin's 40th birthday in a ceremony at Ebenezer Baptist Church. Two days later she formally announced the establishment of the King Center as a nonprofit organization—of which she would serve as chief executive officer—before leaving on a tour of Italy and India. Coretta visited Rome and met Pope Paul at the Vatican. She also received the Italian government's Universal Love Award, becoming the first non-Italian so honored. In India Coretta accepted the Nehru Award on behalf of her husband and then gave a series of speeches in this country that her husband so loved.

In the spring of 1969, Coretta and her sister traveled to London, where Coretta became the first woman to give a sermon at St. Paul's Cathedral—where Martin had give a sermon before accepting his Nobel Peace Prize. She also performed several Freedom Concerts throughout Britain, Germany, and Holland.

Coretta returned home in May. Ralph Abernathy invited her to help lead a strike of black hospital workers organized by Local 1199-B of the Drug and Hospital Union in Charleston,

South Carolina. The majority of the strikers were women who worked as nurse's aides, licensed practical nurses, house-keepers, and laundry workers. Abernathy and the local chapter of the SCLC believed that Coretta's presence would inspire the picketers.

Coretta went to Charleston to aid the striking hospital workers just as her husband had gone to Memphis to help the striking garbage workers the year before. She arrived to find that Ralph Abernathy and several hundred black strikers had been jailed. She gave a speech before 7,000 union supporters at a local church and then led a two-mile march to Charleston Hospital. National Guardsmen were called to keep the protesters in check, but Coretta was not afraid.

The Coretta Scott King Award

Although named for Coretta Scott King, this yearly award—now, in fact, multiple awards—for children's literature was not Coretta's brainchild. In 1969 two school librarians attending the American Library Association (ALA) meeting in New Jersey met at a publisher's promotional booth, vying for a poster of Dr. Martin Luther King, Jr., for their respective school libraries. Mabel McKissick and Glyndon Greer quickly discovered that they shared a love of children's literature, and their conversation soon came around to the fact that African-American authors of children's books had no award to recognize works that focused on African-American subjects. Joining in on their discussion, the publisher whose booth they were visiting, John Carroll, suggested starting an award themselves. From that chance meeting, the Coretta Scott King Award—"designed to commemorate the life and works of Dr. Martin Luther King, Jr., and to honor Mrs. Coretta Scott King for her courage and determination to continue the work for peace and world brotherhood"—was born.

The first CSK Award was given the following year, to Lillie Patterson for her biography *Martin Luther King, Jr.: Man of Peace*. In 1974 the Coretta Scott King Illustrator Award was given for the first time to honor a book's artist as well as its author. That same year, the seal was designed—by Lev Mills of Atlanta—to convey the Kings' belief in peace and brotherhood.

Coretta later served as an honorary chairperson of a committee for the Drug and Hospital Union. She worked with union leaders to make sure the workers' rights were protected.

FULFILLING NEW DREAMS

In September, Coretta's first book, *My Life with Martin Luther King, Jr.*, detailing her life—especially her life with her late husband—was published. Coretta's autobiography was not the only literary high point of her year, however. The American Library Association honored her by establishing the Coretta Scott King Award for outstanding black writers and illustrators of children's literature. Every year since 1969, the award has been given to writers and artists whose work

In 2002 the awards grew again to include the Coretta Scott King/John Steptoe New Author Talent Award and the New Illustrator Talent Award. Past award recipients have included James Haskins for *The Story of Stevie Wonder* (1977); illustrator John Steptoe for both *Mother Crocodile* (1982) and *Mufaro's Beautiful Daughters: An African Tale* (1988); three-time winner Angela Johnson for *Toning the Sweep* (1994), *Heaven* (1999), and *The First Part Last* (2004); and even Coretta Scott King herself, who received a special citation for her book *The Words of Martin Luther King, Jr.* (For a complete list of Coretta Scott King Awards winners, visit the Literature Awards Website: www.literature-awards.com/coretta_scott_king _award.htm.)

Official recognition by the American Library Association didn't come until 1982, but now the ALA proudly promotes the award to "encourage the artistic expression of the African American experience via literature and the graphic arts, including biographical, historical, and social history treatments by African American authors and illustrators."

Although not hands-on regarding the awards that bear her name, Coretta Scott King is nonetheless keenly interested in the spirit behind them and has appeared at the awards ceremony. Certainly she can relate to the notion of visionary inspiration springing from humble beginnings.

exemplifies Dr. King's dream of equality and Coretta's dedication to world peace.

Coretta's involvement with the arts continued at the same time. In 1971, despite her myriad activities and activism, she managed to get her doctorate in music from the New England Conservatory if Music, where she had previously received her master's degree. She also continued to travel, delivering speeches, participating in protests, receiving numerous awards and honors, and networking with powerful people.

After Martin's death, Coretta was elected to the SCLC's board of directors. The alliance between King's widow and the male-dominated SCLC was not an easy one, according to some reports: "Much of our male leadership that honored Dr. King, worshipped Dr. King, find it hard to recognize the strength in a woman like Coretta King," said Dorothy Height, president of the National Council of Negro Women, in an interview with the *Washington Post* 20 years after Martin's death. "It is easier for them to think of her as the widow of a martyr than giving leadership in her own right."

Andrew Young, who worked closely with Dr. King, had no such trouble seeing the steel in Coretta. In an interview with the *Philadelphia Inquirer* in January 2004, he said, "She was always more of an activist than Martin. Although people didn't realize it, the action part was always difficult for him. He wanted to preach and reason things out. Coretta wanted to march."

Coretta had always been outspoken in her own right, but Martin's death had given her a permanent place in the national spotlight. Remembering Ella Baker's words of wisdom, she knew it was her responsibility to speak her mind and move forward with her own vision. To that end, Coretta began to work independently of the SCLC.

Black members of Congress began lobbying their colleagues to support a federal holiday in honor of Martin. Representative John Conyers, Jr., was one of the first congressmen to introduce such a bill, just four days after Martin's assassination. The idea met with little support.

Coretta spearheaded a coalition of politicians, civil-rights advocates, and peace activists in an effort to make Martin's birthday a national holiday. In 1971 the *Washington Post* reported that King's supporters led a mule-drawn wagon to Washington, D.C., and dropped 3 million petitions supporting the holiday on the steps of the Capitol. Congress paid little attention to the demonstration, but Coretta was tireless and continued to travel across the country, calling for a "truly American holiday" that people of every race could celebrate.

Coretta's influence as a civil-rights activist grew steadily during the 1970s. Candidates for national and state office began to seek her endorsement for their campaigns. Governor George McGovern sought her support in his campaign for president, as did black congressional candidate Ron Dellums for his own campaign.

President Jimmy Carter, a great admirer of Coretta's, appointed her as a public delegate to the United Nations. Coretta later cochaired a committee to support the Humphrey-Hawkins Full Employment and Balanced Growth Act, a federal law that stated that every American citizen had the right to a job with decent pay and safe working conditions. Congress later approved the legislation. To combat sexism, Coretta went to Congress to lobby for the passage of the Equal Rights Amendment (ERA) for women.

In 1979 the Martin Luther King, Jr., holiday bill was once again introduced on the floor of Congress, but the measure fell just five votes short of passage. This time Coretta was more determined than ever to get the legislation passed. Several states had already passed their own King holiday bills, but Coretta knew the holiday would have little meaning unless it was observed by the entire nation.

President Carter agreed to approve the legislation if it passed his desk before the end of his term. Despite lobbying

(continued on page 110)

The FBI Files

Thanks to the Freedom of Information Act, the U.S. Department of Justice has opened its files to the public regarding the surveillance of Martin Luther King, Jr.— and to a lesser extent, Coretta Scott King—by the then-director of the FBI, J. Edgar Hoover. Subtitled "FBI Surveillance and Harassment of Dr. King," the files reveal the extent to which Hoover went to bring down a man he considered his nemesis. Famed educator, linguist, and political dissident Noam Chomsky wrote in his *Notes on the State System of Oppression*:

> The commitment of the FBI to undermine the civil-rights movement, despite an elaborate pretense to the contrary . . . will come as no surprise to people with first-hand experience in the South in the early 1960s. As late as summer 1965, FBI observers refused to act within their legal authority to protect civil rights demonstrators who were being savagely beaten by police and thrown into stockades (some who tried to find sanctuary on federal property were thrown from the steps of the federal building in Jackson, Mississippi, be federal marshals).

In fact, the surveillance of Dr. King seems to have stemmed from his criticism of the FBI for not doing enough to protect his and other demonstrators' rights (although some suspect Hoover was jealous of King having won the Nobel Peace Prize). In retaliation, Hoover did his best to prove that the civil-rights leader was a Communist sympathizer with ties to the Communist Party. Hoover approached Attorney General Robert Kennedy with a request to wiretap phones in King's office and home. At first Kennedy turned down the request. According to the report in the FBI's files, however:

> In essence, the Director communicated to Attorney General Kennedy during 1962 and 1963 a host of memoranda concerning the interest of the Communist Party in the civil-rights movement and, in particular, Dr. King's relationship with two frequently consulted advisors whom the FBI had tabbed as members of the Communist Party. As a result of the deep interest in civil-rights affairs by the Attorney General and by the Kennedy Administration, these FBI reports had the effect of alarming Robert Kennedy and affecting his decisions on the national level.

The most egregious exploitation of this surveillance was Hoover's use of a tape compiled from various bugged hotel rooms from the previous two years. The tape was apparently evidence that Dr. King had engaged in numerous extramarital flings. Hoover and his associate director (and longtime companion) Clyde Tolson conspired to blackmail King by threatening to send the embarrassing tape to Coretta and the media if the civil-rights leader didn't commit suicide before the bestowal of the Nobel Prize —which seems to gives credence to the jealousy theory. The unsigned note read:

> King, there is only one thing left for you to do. You know what it is. You have just 34 days in which to do it. (This exact number has been selected for a specific reason.) It has definite practical significance. You are done. There is but one way out for you. You'd better take it before your filthy, abnormal fraudulent self is bared to the nation.

The plot backfired badly, however, when Coretta inadvertently opened the envelope herself. After reading the letter and playing part of the tape, Coretta handed it over to her husband, who clearly did not take Hoover up on his suggestion to kill himself.

As the *St. Louis Post-Dispatch* noted in a November 19, 1975 editorial, "[It is] hard to imagine that there was any tactic too sordid for this federal agency to use." Indeed, the FBI was so eager to discredit Martin Luther King's work that it tried to damage the reputations of his wife and associates, as well. According to the security investigation of the FBI report, after Dr. King's assassination Hoover had Coretta looked at "very closely," including "scrutinizing her travels in an attempt to uncover possible facts embarrassing to her." The FBI director had a plan to leak information to the press that Coretta and Ralph Abernathy plotted to claim that the assassination was a conspiracy, thereby keeping the story in the news "to keep monetary contributions flowing for their benefit."

In the end, it was J. Edgar Hoover who ended up discredited.

(continued from page 107)

hard for the bill, Coretta and her allies faced staunch political opponents—most notably Senators Strom Thurmond and Jesse Helms—who questioned whether Martin's achievements merited honoring him with a national holiday. In the end, the senators won—that time.

The King holiday campaign was one of the most popular public endeavors in recent history. In 1980 Grammy Award-winning singer and musician Stevie Wonder wrote a song called "Happy Birthday," which became the anthem for the crusade. In that same year, the U.S. National Park Service declared Dr. King's childhood home and the surrounding neighborhood on Auburn Avenue a historic district to preserve the area. Encouraged, Coretta and the King Center staff started another petition drive to support the King holiday. Coretta was not going to give up.

To commemorate the twentieth anniversary of the March on Washington, the King Center sponsored a new Coalition of Conscience, which brought together hundreds of human-rights organizations, to advocate a 12-point plan to promote jobs, peace, and freedom. A proposal for the King holiday was part of the plan. Standing on the steps of the Lincoln Memorial on August 28, 1983, where her husband had stood 20 years before, Coretta and the leaders of other civil-rights and peace groups reiterated Martin's call for social justice. This time 500,000 people publicly showed their support for a national holiday in honor of Dr. King. As Martin's birthday anthem filled the air, Coretta clapped and sang along, hoping that President Ronald Reagan and Congress were listening.

Three months later, on November 2, Coretta went to the White House to watch President Reagan sign legislation that established the third Monday in January as the official celebration of the birthday of the Reverend Dr. Martin Luther King, Jr. Senator Helms, however, still opposed the King holiday. He alleged that Dr. King had affiliations with the Communist Party USA during the civil-rights movement and

Coretta stands behind President Ronald Reagan as he signs a bill making Martin's birthday a national holiday.

questioned King's allegiance to the U.S. government. To prove his allegations, Helms wanted to examine sealed FBI files on King, but a judge refused his request.

Several weeks before signing the bill, President Reagan, who at first opposed the holiday, commented in a press conference that he did not fault Senator Helms for "wanting the records opened up" to investigate Dr. King's alleged affiliations with the Communist Party. The president's statement caused many black leaders to question his support for civil rights. Later, the president reportedly called Coretta to apologize for his statement at the press conference.

As she witnessed the signing, Coretta Scott King smiled while several other black leaders and civil-rights colleagues sang "We Shall Overcome." She had proven over the years that she had the will, foresight, and know-how to keep her husband's legacy alive.

10

The Dream Continues

January 15, 1986, marked the first official national holiday honoring Dr. Martin Luther King, Jr. Coretta and her four children celebrated the historic occasion at the King Center and sponsored a program called "Ending the Violence of Poverty, World Hunger, and Apartheid Through Creative Nonviolent Actions." Coretta also led the first Martin Luther King, Jr., Day march though the streets of Atlanta. From this day forward, Americans would remember Dr. King's lifelong commitment to the full equality of all human beings.

In 1988 Coretta was named chairperson of the Martin Luther King, Jr., Federal Holiday Commission, which would coordinate celebration activities in communities across the nation. At the time, Coretta told journalist Barbara Reynolds, "We promote [Martin Luther King Day] as a holiday for people of all races, religions, and color[s]. I would be disappointed if it turned out to be a black holiday. [Martin] was all inclusive."

IN SERVICE TO OTHERS

Of course, Coretta's work with the King Center was her primary focus. By the time of the first observance of Martin Luther King Day, the King Center was already an established institution.

The King Center opened its doors to the public in 1982. Since then, more than one million people from around the world have visited the historic site each year. Coretta's fundraising efforts to build the center have been extraordinary, with more than $10 million in contributions reportedly collected. The center now includes an interdenominational chapel, exhibit halls, seminar rooms, a 250-seat auditorium, and an international conference and cultural center capable of translating numerous languages. Workshops on conflict resolution, nonviolent protest techniques, and community development are also held.

Coretta's achievements have not been solely King-centric. In 1984 she took up the cause of apartheid, doing battle with the oppressive all-white South-African government that had ruled black Africans with an iron fist since 1910. Blacks were not allowed to own land or live in cities. They were segregated in barren, overcrowded areas called "homelands." They worked at menial, low-paying jobs; had to send their children to dismal schools; and, of course, did not have the right to vote. Nelson Mandela, a black-African lawyer, helped lead a freedom movement in South Africa during the late 1950s and early 1960s. Arrested in 1964, he was given a life sentence by the government on charges of treason.

Coretta was especially drawn to the South African freedom struggle because Mandela and his wife at the time, Winnie, appeared to walk the same path that she and Martin had traveled during their years together. Coretta and scores of other human rights activists in the United States and around the world participated in demonstrations to protest the South African government's policies and Mandela's imprisonment.

In 1984 the United Nations Special Committee Against Apartheid invited Coretta to be the keynote speaker at its International Day of Solidarity with the Women of South Africa and Namibia. A year later she and three of her children were arrested during a protest in front of the South African Embassy in Washington, D.C. Then in 1988 the King Center sent a delegation to South Africa on a fact-finding mission to document evidence of racial discrimination and government repression.

International trade sanctions and political pressures against apartheid, coupled with decades of bloody violence, finally broke the back of the South African government. In 1990 South African President F.W. de Klerk released Nelson Mandela from prison. By then Mandela had earned the admiration of the entire world. His people saw him as a symbol of hope in desperate times—just as black Americans had come to regard Martin Luther King, Jr.

Four years later, on April 27, 1994, the black majority of South Africa exercised its newly won right to vote in their nation's first nonracial government election. On May 2, 1994, Coretta stood on a podium in South Africa with newly elected President Nelson Mandela, who had defeated President de Klerk and become the leader of South Africa. The South African freedom movement had come full circle. Coretta Scott King had done her part to help make that day happen.

World peace was still very much on Coretta's mind. In 1988, in preparation for the summit between President Ronald Reagan and Soviet leader Mikhail Gorbachev, Coretta headed the U.S. delegation of Women for a Meaningful Summit, held in Athens, Greece. Then two years later, Coretta served as cochair of the Soviet-American Women's Summit in Washington.

Perhaps one of the most historic events that Coretta attended took place in 1993. She was invited to the White House by President Bill Clinton to witness the signing of the Middle East Peace Accords and the historic handshake

Coretta sits with her son Dexter at a service commemorating Martin's life. Dexter followed in Coretta's footsteps, heading the King Center after Coretta stepped down.

between Israeli Prime Minister Yitzhak Rabin and Palestinian Chairman Yassir Arafat. Over the years Coretta has also met with such spiritual leaders as the Dalai Lama, Bishop Desmond Tutu, and Catholic activist Dorothy Day.

Today, Coretta Scott King can look back proudly on a lifetime of social service and commitment. She also almost single-handedly raised four children who are now productive adults. Yolanda is an actress and film producer; Martin III is a businessman in Atlanta; Bernice, who holds both a doctorate of law degree and a master of divinity degree, is a pastor at the Greater Rising Star Baptist Church, also in Atlanta; and Dexter Scott now heads up the King Center.

PASSING THE TORCH

In October 1995, after 27 years, Coretta stepped down as CEO and president of the Martin Luther King, Jr., Center for Nonviolent Social Change and handed the reins of leadership to her son. It was not easy for Coretta to pass the King legacy on to her son. "I wanted to, but it was hard to let go," Coretta told *Ebony* magazine. "The children refer to the Center as my fifth child. But once I made the decision, I felt relief and inner peace."

DID YOU KNOW?

For years Coretta Scott King has tackled the issue of homophobia in America, believing that injustice and intolerance are the same, no matter what form it comes in or what group is targeted. "For many years now I have been an outspoken supporter of civil and human rights for gay and lesbian people," she told a crowd assembled for the Lambda Legal Defense and Education Fund in 1998. "Homophobia is like racism and anti-Semitism and other forms of bigotry in that it seeks to dehumanize a large group of people, to deny their humanity, their dignity and personhood." Believing that parallels to the civil-rights movement can be seen in the gay-rights movement, she stated, "Freedom from discrimination based on sexual orientation is surely a fundamental human right in any great democracy, as much as freedom from racial, religious, gender, or ethnic discrimination."

Coretta also criticizes black homophobia, blaming this attitude for the high incidence of HIV and AIDS in the African-American population. "I have no doubt that homophobia has worsened and prolonged the AIDS crisis. It is sad to me when I hear black people, including some in leadership positions, making homophobic comments and attacking the human rights of gay and lesbian people," she told the *Atlanta Journal-Constitution* in October 1999. "African Americans have suffered for too long because of prejudice and bigotry to be parroting the rhetoric of the Ku Klux Klan and other hate groups who bash people because of their sexual orientation."

Coretta still accepts numerous speaking engagements and continues to lead a busy—although more private—life. She has worked extensively with Sarah and Jim Brady for the cause of handgun control. She also has addressed the problems of HIV and AIDS in the black community, as well as taking a strong stand for gay and lesbian rights.

Of course, simply being Coretta Scott King guarantees that she will always be in the public eye to some degree.

UNRESOLVED QUESTIONS

Since the assassination of Martin Luther King, Jr., in 1968, mystery has surrounded the man convicted for the crime, James Earl Ray. Although Ray—who was an escaped convict at the time of the shooting—pleaded guilty to King's murder before the case ever got to court, he later recanted his confession. He died of liver disease in 1998, still serving his 99-year sentence and still swearing to his innocence. The U.S. Justice Department reopened the investigation, studying Coretta's collection of evidence, which she had amassed over the years, that supported the theory of a conspiracy. After seven months of testimony and deliberation, however, a Memphis district attorney concluded that it appeared Ray had indeed acted alone.

Dissatisfied with this ruling, the King family filed a wrongful-death suit against a man who said he was paid to plan the assassination. In December 1999, a jury concluded that Martin Luther King, Jr., had been assassinated by "a conspiracy involving Lloyd Jowers (who formerly owned the restaurant that overlooked the motel where King had been shot) and others, including governmental agencies."

"If we know the truth, we can be free to go on with our lives," Coretta testified at the time. Unfortunately, that truth may never actually be known.

A LIFE WELL LIVED

Coretta Scott King has lived out most of her adult life in the

Coretta speaks at a news conference at the King Center following the jury verdict concluding that Martin's assassination was the result of a conspiracy, not the actions of a single gunman.

public eye, yet at the same time she has been something of an enigma. An extremely independent and strong-willed woman, she often made huge concessions to her paternalistic—some might say chauvinistic—husband. Instead of the concert career she had studied and worked so hard for, her primary role while Martin was alive was that of wife and mother. She never remarried after her husband's murder and dated only occasionally. Ironically, it was only after becoming a widow that Coretta truly came into her own.

Through both great tragedy and great triumph, Coretta has always been notable for her dignity and her strength—so much so that the real woman often seems hidden from view. It is as a woman, not a legend, that Coretta Scott King would like most to be remembered, however. As she told a standing-room-only crowd that had come to hear her speak at California University of Pennsylvania on January 28, 2003, "I am often identified as the widow of Martin Luther King, Jr. Sometimes I am also identified as a civil-rights leader or a human-rights activist. While these designations are factually correct, I would also like to be thought of as a complex, three-dimensional, flesh-and-blood human being with a rich storehouse of experiences, much like everyone else yet unique in my own way . . . much like everyone else."

1927 Born Coretta Scott in Heiberger, Alabama

1945 Graduates as valedictorian from segregated Lincoln High School; enters Antioch College on scholarship

1951 Graduates from Antioch; enters New England Conservatory of Music

1952 Meets Martin Luther King, Jr.

1953 Marries Martin Luther King, Jr., in Marion, Alabama

1954 Graduates from New England Conservatory of Music; moves to Montgomery, Alabama, with Martin

1955 Gives birth to Yolanda Denise King; Montgomery bus boycott begins

1956 King home is firebombed; racial segregation on Montgomery buses is declared unconstitutional; Coretta stages a concert to raise funds for the Montgomery Improvement Association (MIA)

1957 Standing in for Martin, Coretta attends a meeting of black ministers in Atlanta; the Southern Christian Leadership Conference (SCLC) is formed at a follow-up meeting in New Orleans; son Martin Luther King III is born

1958 Makes first solo public speaking appearance on Women's Day at New Hope Baptist Church in Denver, Colorado; Martin is stabbed in Harlem

1959 Travels to India with Martin

1960 Moves to Atlanta with Martin; joins Women's International League for Peace and Freedom

1961 Gives birth to Dexter Scott King

1962 Travels to Geneva, Switzerland, as part of an international delegation of 50 women to lobby for a ban on atomic-weapons testing

1963 Gives birth to Bernice Albertine King; participates in the March on Washington for Jobs and Freedom; President John F. Kennedy is assassinated

1964 Performs the first in a series of Freedom Concerts to raise funds for the SCLC's civil-rights causes; accompanies Martin to Oslo, Norway, where he receives the Nobel Peace Prize

1965 Enrolls her two oldest children in a previously all-white public school in Atlanta

1966 Moves with family to a public housing unit in Chicago as part of a campaign against urban poverty; helps found Women Mobilized for Change to help city residents improve their living conditions

1968 Martin is assassinated in Memphis, Tennessee; Coretta appears in his place on Solidarity Day at the Lincoln Memorial, making a historic speech of her own; announces plans to build Martin Luther King Center for Nonviolent Social Change

1969 Travels to Italy and India; receives Italian government's Universal Love Award and visits the Vatican; accepts India's Nehru Award on behalf of Martin; visits England and becomes first woman to give sermon at St. Paul's Cathedral in London; leads striking hospital workers on march in Charleston, South Carolina; Coretta's autobiography, *My Life with Martin Luther King, Jr.*, is published; American Library Association establishes Coretta Scott King Book Award for children's literature

1982 Opens Martin Luther King Center for Nonviolent Social Change to the public

1983 Attends signing ceremony as President Ronald Reagan makes Martin Luther King's birthday a national holiday

1986 Leads King holiday march in Atlanta to mark first
        official observance

1990 Welcomes Nelson Mandela to America during a rally in
        Atlanta after his release from prison

1994 Steps down as CEO and president of King Center;
        appoints son Dexter to replace her

1997 Coretta and children publicly support motion for retrial
        of convicted King assassin James Earl Ray; the King
        family files a wrongful-death suit against Lloyd Jowers

1999 The King family wins a wrongful-death civil suit against
        Lloyd Jowers

Dyson, Michael Eric. *I May Not Get There with You: The True Martin Luther King, Jr.* New York: Simon & Schuster, 2000.

Garrow, David J. "Pointing Toward a Plot." *Newsweek*, February 17, 1997, 55.

———. *Bearing the Cross: Martin Luther King, Jr. and the Southern Christian Leadership Conference.* New York: William Morrow, 1986.

Giddings, Paula. *When and Where I Enter: The Impact of Black Women on Race and Sex in America.* New York: William Morrow, 1984.

Harris, Art. "Carrying on the Dream." *Washington Post*, January 19, 1986.

Jones, Malcolm Jr. "A Multimedia 'Dream.'" *Newsweek*, January 20, 1997, 66.

King, Coretta Scott. *My Life with Martin Luther King, Jr.* Rev. ed. New York: Henry Holt and Company, 1993.

Patterson, Lillie. *Coretta Scott King.* Easton, MD: Garrard Publishing Company, 1977.

Vivian, Octavia. *Coretta: The Story of Mrs. Martin Luther King, Jr.* Philadelphia: Fortress Press, 1970.

White, Jack E. "The Mysteries of James Earl Ray." *Time*, February 17, 1997, 73.

Williams, Juan. "Coretta's Way." *Washington Post*, June 4, 1989.

The Words of Martin Luther King, Jr. Selected by Coretta Scott King. New York: Newmarket Press, 1983.

WEBSITES

American Library Association. "Coretta Scott King Book Awards."
www.ala.org/ala/srrt/corettascottking/corettascott.htm

FBI Files: Freedom of Information Act, File #106670, Main File Section 103.
http://foia.fbi.gov/foiaindex/king.htm

Abernathy, Juanita, 3, 51, 87,
    90
Abernathy, Ralph
  and arrested in Birmingham,
    79
  and arrested in Selma, 87
  and children in previously
    all-white school, 90
  and Coretta as speaker, 70
  and march to Selma, 89
  and Martin arrested for traffic
    violation, 56
  and Martin's assassination, 2,
    8–9
  and Martin's stabbing, 68
  and Memphis sanitation
    workers' march, 10
  and Montgomery bus boycott,
    54, 55, 60, 62, 63
  and Montgomery Improvement
    Association, 69
  in Norway for Martin's Nobel
    Peace Prize, 87
  as pastor at First Baptist
    Church in Montgomery, 51,
    57
  and Southern Christian Leader-
    ship Conference, 10, 101–102,
    103–104
  and strike of black hospital
    workers in Charleston, South
    Carolina, 103–104
  and voter registration drive,
    74
Alabama
  and Coretta attending school
    and living in Marion,
    20–22
  and Coretta's early years in
    Heiberger, 14–24
  and Martin arrested in Selma,
    87–88

  and voter registration drive in
    Marion, 87–89
  and voter registration drive in
    Selma, 87–88.
    See also Birmingham, Alabama;
    Montgomery, Alabama
Allen, Ivan, Jr., 3–4
American Library Association,
  and Coretta Scott King Award,
    105–106
Anderson, Walter, 29, 34
Antioch College (Yellow Springs,
  Ohio), 25
  Coretta attending, 27–34
  Coretta's sister attending,
    25–27, 29–30
  racism at, 29–33
apartheid, Coretta involved with,
    113–114
Arafat, Yassir, 115
Atlanta, Georgia
  and Bernice King as pastor at
    Greater Rising Star Baptist
    Church, 115
  and Coretta and Martin
    moving to Atlanta, 69
  and integration of public
    schools, 89–90
  and King children in previously
    all-white school, 89–90
  Southern Christian Leadership
    Conference in, 8, 10, 64–65,
    69.
  See also Ebenezer Baptist
    Church (Atlanta)

Baker, Ella, 70, 106
Bartol, Mrs., 34, 36
Belafonte, Harry, 7, 9, 62,
    100–101
Bennett, Mattie, 19–20
Bennette, Fred, Jr., 4

Birmingham, Alabama
  Abernathy arrested in, 79
  and bombing of Sixteenth
    Street Baptist Church, 84
  and Children's Crusade,
    79–81
  Martin arrested in, 79
  and Southern Christian
    Leadership Conference fight
    for desegregation, 77–81
"Black Madonna," Coretta as,
  99
Black Muslims, 87
Black Panthers, 95
Black Power, 95
Bloody Sunday, 89
Boston University, and Martin
  attending School of Theology,
  37, 44, 45, 49, 52
Brady, Sarah and Jim, 117
Brown v. Board of Education of
  Topeka, Kansas, 48–49, 81
buses, and Montgomery bus
  boycott, 52–62

Carmichael, Stokely, 95
Carter, Jimmy, 107, 110
Chicago, Illinois
  Coretta and Martin moving
    to, 90, 92
  housing for blacks in, 90,
    92–94
  money for blacks in, 94
Children's Crusade, 79–81
church, in South, 16, 19
cities
  and Poor People's Campaign,
    90, 92–94, 95–96, 101–102
  riots in, 95
Civil Rights Act of 1957, 77
Civil Rights Act of 1964, 85, 89,
  90

Civil War, 17, 49
civil-rights movement, beginning
  of, 55
Clark, Jim, 88
Clinton, Bill, 114
Coalition of Conscience,
  110
Communist Party, Martin's
  alleged affiliations with,
  110–111
Connor, Eugene "Bull," 77, 79,
  80, 81
Constitution, and Fourteenth
  Amendment, 49
Conyers, John, 106–107
Cosby, Bill, 7
cotton, Coretta picking,
  17, 19
Crozer Seminary
  (Pennsylvania), Martin
  attending, 37
Culp, Robert, 7
Curry, Isola, 68

Dalai Lama, 115
Daley, Richard, 92, 93
Day, Dorothy, 115
de Klerk, F.W., 114
Dean, Arthur, 73–74
Dellums, Ron, 107
Dexter Avenue Baptist Church
  (Montgomery, Alabama)
  Coretta in choir at, 52
  Martin as pastor at, 49,
    50, 52
Drug and Hospital Union
  (Charleston, South Carolina)
  and Coretta as honorary chair-
    person, 105
  and Coretta leading strike of
    black hospital workers,
    103–104

Easter, Martin assassinated week
    before, 1–2, 4–6
Ebenezer Baptist Church
    (Atlanta), 64
    Coretta addressing Martin's
        followers after assassination
        in, 10
    Coretta celebrating Martin's
        40th birthday in, 103
    Martin as assistant pastor at,
        37, 44, 69
    Martin as pastor at, 10
    Martin's father as pastor at, 37,
        40–41
    Martin's funeral in, 11–12,
        99
Ebony magazine, 101, 116
Edmund Pettus Bridge, 88–89
Eisenhower, Dwight, and Southern
    Christian Leadership Conference,
    64–65
Ellington, Duke, 62
Emancipation Proclamation,
    17
England, Coretta in, 86–87, 103
Equal Rights Amendment
    (ERA), 107
Essence magazine, 77–78
Europe, Coretta and Martin in,
    66
Evers, Medgar, 84

Farris, Christine King (sister-in-
    law), 4
Farris, Isaac (brother-in-law), 4
FBI, and bugging Martin's tele-
    phones and hotel rooms, 6–7
First Baptist Church (Montgomery,
    Alabama)
    Abernathy as pastor at, 51
    and firebombing, 64
Fourteenth Amendment, 49

Freedom Concerts, Coretta giving,
    62, 66, 68–69, 86, 89, 103
Freedom Rides, 72
Friendly Inn Settlement House,
    Coretta working at, 28
Funtown amusement park,
    76–77

Gandhi, Mahatma, 42, 64
Garrow, David, 53–54
Geneva, Switzerland, Coretta
    fighting for world peace in,
    73–75
Georgia, and voter registration
    drive in Albany, 74.
    See also Atlanta, Georgia
Ghana, Coretta and Martin in,
    65–66
Gorbachev, Mikhail, 114
Gray, Fred D., 55
Great Depression, 16, 17
Greater Rising Star Baptist
    Church (Atlanta), Bernice King
    as pastor at, 115

Hanley's Funeral Home
    (Atlanta), Martin's body taken
    to, 7
"Happy Birthday" (song), 110
Harlem (New York)
    Malcolm X assassinated in, 88
    Martin stabbed in, 67–68
Harlem Hospital, Martin in after
    stabbing, 67–68
Height, Dorothy, 106
Helms, Jesse, 110, 110–111
Hoover, J. Edgar, and bugging
    Martin's telephones and hotel
    rooms, 6–7
Humphrey-Hawkins Full
    Employment and Balanced
    Growth Act, 107

I Spy (television show), 7
India
    Coretta in, 68–69, 103
    Martin in, 68–69
International Day of Solidarity
    with the Women of South
    Africa and Namibia, 114
Italy, Coretta in, 66, 103

Jackson, Jesse
    and Martin's assassination, 2,
        3, 8
    and Operation Breadbasket,
        94
Jackson, Jimmie Lee, 88
Jet magazine, 66
Johnson, Lyndon B., 6, 85, 89
Jowers, Lloyd, 117

Karamu Camp, and Coretta as
    junior music counselor, 28
Kennedy, Jacqueline, 99
Kennedy, John F., 6
    and assassination, 84–85
    and Birmingham desegregation
        battle, 80
    and civil-rights legislation, 77,
        81, 85
    and funeral, 99
    and Martin in Birmingham jail,
        79
    and Martin released from
        Reidsville, Georgia jail,
        6, 71
    and voter registration drive in
        Albany, Georgia, 74
Kennedy, Robert
    and civil-rights legislation,
        77
    and King's assassination, 6–7
    and Martin in Birmingham
        jail, 79

    and Martin released from
        Reidsville, Georgia jail, 6, 71
    and Martin's hotel rooms and
        telephones bugged, 6–7
King, Alberta Williams (mother-
    in-law), 40, 44, 60
King, Alfred Daniel ("A.D.")
    (brother-in-law), 40, 80
King, Bernice ("Bunny") (daugh-
    ter), 3, 6, 7, 77–78, 102, 115
King, Christine (sister-in-law),
    40, 68
King, Coretta Scott
    and addressing Martin's
        supporters after assassination,
        9, 10
    and apartheid, 113–114
    and autobiography, 103, 105
    birth of, 14
    as "Black Madonna," 99
    and bringing Martin's body
        back to Atlanta, 7
    childhood of, 14–21
    and children in previously
        all-white school, 89–90
    children of, 1, 2, 3, 6, 7, 9, 10,
        11, 52, 55, 57, 66, 71, 73,
        75–78, 85, 89–90, 100, 101,
        112, 115
    and Coalition of Conscience,
        110
    criticism of, 94–95
    education of, 17, 19–20, 25,
        27–34, 36, 38, 43, 44, 45, 49,
        106
    in England, 86–87, 103
    family of, 14–24, 25–27
    and financial security after
        Martin's death, 100–101
    and Freedom Concerts, 62, 66,
        68–69, 86, 89, 103
    and Freedom Rides, 72

and gay and lesbian rights, 117
in Ghana, 65–66
and handgun control, 117
and HIV and AIDS, 117
and honors and awards, 103, 105–106
as house cleaner, 22, 36
and housing for blacks in Chicago, 90, 92, 93
in India, 68–69, 103
in Italy, 66, 103
and Kennedy's assassination, 84–85, 99
and King Center for Nonviolent Social Change, 102–103, 110, 112, 113, 115, 116
and leading Memphis sanitation workers' march, 9–11, 101
and leading striking hospital workers in Charleston, South Carolina, 103–104
and living in Marion, Alabama, 20–22
and Malcolm X, 87–88
and march from Selma to Montgomery, 89
and March on Washington for Jobs and Freedom, 81, 83, 110
and marriage, 38–45. *See also* King, Martin Luther, Jr.
and Martin stabbed in Harlem, 67–68
and Martin winning Nobel Peace Prize, 9, 86–87
and Martin's arrests, 70–71, 79
and Martin's assassination, 1–9, 96, 97–98, 117
and Martin's birthday as national holiday, 106–107, 110–111, 112–113
and Martin's funeral, 9–10, 11–13, 99–100
and Martin's sermon in St. Paul's Cathedral (London), 86–87
and Mexican vacation, 66
and Middle East Peace Accords, 114–115
and Montgomery bus boycott, 54, 55–59, 61–62, 63
and move to Atlanta, 69
and move to Chicago, 90, 92
and move to Montgomery, 49–51
and music, 16–17, 20, 21, 22, 27, 28–29, 30, 32–33, 34, 36, 38, 40, 43, 44, 45, 47, 49–50, 52, 62, 68–69, 86, 89, 103, 106
and mystery over Martin's assassination, 117
in Nigeria, 66
and nonviolent protest, 9, 59, 60, 87, 94–95, 102, 112
and peace movement, 13, 69, 73–75, 94, 101, 102, 114–115
and personality, 17
and picking cotton, 17, 19
and political involvement, 107, 110, 114–115, 117
and Poor People's Campaign, 101–102
and public speaking, 66, 69–70, 89, 93, 94, 101–102, 106, 110, 114, 117, 119
racism experienced by, 21–22, 29–33, 45
and religion, 9, 22, 32–33, 100
and sermon at St. Paul's Cathedral (London), 103
and Solidarity Day, 101–102
and Southern Christian Leadership Conference, 64, 69, 86, 106
and values, 18, 42
and Vietnam War, 94

and voter registration drives, 66, 69, 85, 87, 89
as widow, 9–11, 99–107, 110–117
as wife to Martin, 1, 45, 47, 58–59
and Women Mobilized for Change, 93
King, Coretta Scott, Award, 105–106
King, Dexter (son), 3, 6, 7, 10, 11, 76, 102, 115
King, Martin Luther, III (son), 3, 6, 7, 10, 11, 66, 76, 89–90, 102, 115
King, Martin Luther, Jr. (husband)
and arrests, 6, 60–61, 70–71, 79, 87–88
and assassination, 1–9, 96, 97–98, 117
as assistant pastor at Ebenezer Baptist Church, 37, 44, 69
as Baptist minister, 10, 37, 38–39, 43, 44, 47, 49, 50, 52, 69
and Birmingham desegregation battle, 77–81
birth of, 40
and birthday as national holiday, 106–107, 110–111, 112–113
childhood of, 40–42
children of, 2, 3, 52, 55, 57, 66, 71, 73–75, 77–78, 85, 89–90, 92
and civil rights legislation, 77, 85
and Communist Party, 110–111
criticism of, 94–95
and dating Coretta, 42–44
and education, 12, 37, 38, 40, 41–42, 44, 45, 49, 52
and engaged to other woman, 43, 44
in England, 86–87
family of, 40–42

and FBI bugging telephones and hotel rooms, 6–7
and Freedom Rides, 72
and funeral, 9–10, 11–13, 99–100
and Gandhi, 42
in Ghana, 65–66
and home and neighborhood as historic district, 110
and housing for blacks in Chicago, 90, 92–94
as husband, 1, 9, 45, 47, 58–59
in India, 68–69
and indicted for falsifying income tax returns, 69
and Kennedy's assassination, 84–85
and march from Selma to Montgomery, 89
and March on Washington for Jobs and Freedom, 81, 83
and marriage to Coretta, 44–45
and meeting Coretta, 38–40
and Memphis sanitation workers' march, 1, 2, 10–11, 96–98
and Mexican vacation, 66
and Montgomery bus boycott, 54, 55–61, 62, 63
and Montgomery Improvement Association, 54, 55, 62, 64, 69
and move to Atlanta, 69
and move to Chicago, 90, 92
and move to Montgomery, 49–51
and mystery over assassination, 117
in Nigeria, 66
and Nobel Peace Prize, 9, 86–87
and nonviolent protest, 3, 9, 13, 42, 49, 64, 72, 74–75, 94–95, 97, 100
as pastor at Dexter Avenue Baptist Church, 49, 50, 52

and pastor at Ebenezer Baptist Church, 10

and personality, 38, 40

and Poor People's Campaign, 90, 92–94, 95–96

racism experienced by, 41–42, 45

and sermon in St. Paul's Cathedral (London), 86–87

and sit-ins, 70–71, 72, 74

and Southern Christian Leadership Conference, 8, 10, 64, 69, 71

and stabbed in Harlem, 67–68

and Student Nonviolent Coordinating Committee, 70

and values, 42

and Vietnam War, 94

and voter registration drives, 66, 69, 74, 85, 87–89

and writings, 66–67

King, Martin Luther, Jr., Center for Nonviolent Social Change Coretta heading, 102–103, 110, 112, 113

Dexter King heading, 115, 116

King, Martin Luther, Jr., Day, 106–107, 110–111, 112–113

King, Martin Luther, Jr., Federal Holiday Commission, 112

King, Martin Luther, Sr. ("Daddy King") (father-in-law), 6, 10, 40, 40–41, 42, 43, 44, 45, 58, 60

King, Yolanda Denise ("Yoki") (daughter), 2, 3, 7, 8, 10, 11, 52, 55, 57, 71, 76, 77, 85, 89–90, 102, 115

Ku Klux Klan, 70

Kyles, Samuel B., 8

Lincoln, Abraham, 17

Lincoln High School (Marion, Alabama)
Coretta attending, 20–22

Coretta singing at, 33

Coretta's brother attending, 21

Coretta's sister attending, 20–21

Lorraine Motel (Memphis)
and Martin shot on balcony, 2, 7–9, 98

and Poor People's Campaign, 101

Luther, Martin, 92

lynching, 18

McDonald, Dora, 2, 3, 4

McGovern, George, 107

McMurry, Martin (maternal grandfather), 16, 19, 22

Malcolm X, 87–88

Mandela, Nelson, 113, 114

Mandela, Winnie, 113

Mann, Horace, 25

March on Washington for Jobs and Freedom, and Coretta and Martin, 81, 82, 110

Marquette Park (Chicago), 93

Marshall, Thurgood, 49

Massachusetts
and Coretta attending New England Conservatory of Music in Boston, 34, 36, 38, 43, 44, 45, 49, 106

and Martin attending Boston University, 37, 44, 45, 49, 52

Mays, Benjamin, 13, 37, 38

Memphis, Tennessee
and Martin's assassination, 1–2, 97–98

and sanitation workers' march, 1, 8, 9–11, 96–98, 101

Mexico, Coretta and Martin on vacation in, 66

Middle East Peace Accords, Coretta witnessing, 114–115

Montgomery, Alabama
and bus boycott, 52–62, 63, 64, 65
and church firebombings, 64
and Civil War, 49
Coretta and Martin moving to, 49–51
and King home firebombed, 2, 56–58
and march from Selma, 88–89
and Martin arrested in bus boycott, 60–61
and Martin as pastor in Dexter Avenue Baptist Church, 49, 50, 52
and Montgomery Improvement Association, 54, 55, 62, 64, 69
and voter registration drive, 69

Montgomery Improvement Association (MIA), 54, 55, 62, 64

Morehouse College (Atlanta)
Martin attending, 12, 37, 38, 40
Martin's funeral at, 12–13

Mount Tabor A.M.E. (African Methodist Episcopal) Zion Church (Heiberger, Alabama), Coretta's family attending, 16

My Life with Martin Luther King, Jr. (autobiography), 103, 105

Nation of Islam, 95

National Association for the Advancement of Colored People (NAACP)
and assassination of Evers, 84
and Brown v. Board of Education, 48–49
Coretta joining in college, 32
and Montgomery bus boycott, 54

Nehru Award, Coretta receiving on behalf of Martin, 103

New England Conservatory of Music (Boston, Massachusetts), Coretta attending, 34, 36, 38, 43, 44, 45, 49, 106

New Hope Baptist Church (Denver), Coretta's public speaking debut in, 66

New York, Coretta at peace rally in, 13.
See also Harlem (New York)

New York Times, The, 102

Newton, Huey P., 95

Nigeria, Coretta and Martin in, 66

Nixon, E.D., 54, 62

Nkrumah, Kwame, 65

Nobel Peace Prize, Martin winning, 9, 86–87

nonviolent movement, 3, 9, 13, 42, 49, 64, 72, 74–75

nonviolent protest
and Coretta, 9, 59, 60, 87, 94–95, 102, 112
and Martin, 3, 9, 13, 42, 49, 64, 72, 74–75, 94–95, 97, 100

Norway, Coretta and Martin in for his Nobel Peace Prize, 86–87

Noyes, Jessie Smith, Foundation, Coretta's scholarship from, 34

nuclear testing, Coretta lobbying for ban on, 73–75

Ohio
and Coretta and sister attending Antioch College in Yellow Springs, 25–34
and Coretta's sister attending Ohio State University, 30

Olav V, 87

Operation Breadbasket, 94

Parks, Rosa, 52–54, 55, 60, 61, 62
Paul IV, Pope, 86, 94, 103
Philadelphia Inquirer, 106
Poor People's Campaign, 90,
    92–94, 95–96, 101–102
Powell, Mary, 38, 44

Rabin, Yitzhak, 115
Race Relations and Civil Liberties
    committees, Coretta joining in
    college, 32
Ray, James Earl, 117
Reagan, Ronald, 110, 114
Reynolds, Barbara, 112
Rich's Department Store
    (Atlanta), sit-in at, 70
Robeson, Paul, 29
Rustin, Bayard, 64

St. Joseph's Hospital (Memphis),
    Martin in, 2–3, 4
St. Paul's Cathedral (London)
    Coretta giving sermon in, 103
    Martin giving sermon in, 86–87
sanitation workers' march
    (Memphis), 1, 8, 9–11, 96–98,
    101
satyagraha, 42
school segregation, end of,
    48–49, 81
Scott, Bernice McMurry
    (mother)
    children of, 15–16
    and Coretta's education, 20, 27
    and Coretta's sister's education,
        25–27
    and farm, 15, 16
    and haircutting, 16
    and influence on Coretta, 18
    and marriage, 15
    and religion, 16, 19
    as school bus driver, 22

Scott, Cora (paternal grand-
    mother), 14
Scott, Edythe (sister), 15, 103
    education of, 19–21, 25–27,
        29–30
Scott, Jeff (paternal grandfather),
    14, 16, 18–19
Scott, Obadiah (father), 14
    as barber, 16, 17
    children of, 15–16
    and Coretta's education, 27
    and Coretta's marriage to
        Martin, 44–45
    and Coretta's sister's education,
        25–27
    and farm, 15, 16
    and general merchandise store,
        34
    and hauling lumber in own
        trucks, 16, 17, 22, 23
    and influence on Coretta, 18,
        22–24
    and marriage, 15
    and new home, 22–23
    and owning sawmill, 23
    and racism, 16, 18, 22–24,
        31–32
    and religion, 16, 19
    and sawmill worker, 16
    and wanting Coretta to leave
        danger of Montgomery, 58
Scott, Obie (brother), 15–16, 17
Second Baptist Church (Spring-
    field, Ohio), Coretta's singing
    debut in, 32–33
Shaw University (Raleigh, North
    Carolina), and Student Nonvio-
    lent Coordinating Committee,
    70
sit-ins, 70–71, 72, 74
Sixteenth Street Baptist Church
    (Birmingham), bombing of, 84

slavery, 17–18
Solidarity Day march, 101–102
South Africa, and Coretta
  involved with apartheid,
  113–114
South Carolina, and Coretta
  leading black hospital workers'
  strike in Charleston, 103–104
Southern Christian Leadership
  Conference (SCLC)
  and Abernathy, 10, 101–102,
    103–104
  and Birmingham desegregation
    battle, 77–81
  and Children's Crusade, 79–81
  and civil rights legislation, 77
  and Coretta on board of
    directors, 106
  Coretta raising money for, 86
  and Eisenhower, 64–65
  formation of, 64
  and march from Selma to
    Montgomery, 88–89
  and Martin in jail, 71
  and Martin's assassination, 10
  and Memphis sanitation workers'
    march, 1, 8, 9–11, 96–98
  and money for blacks in
    Chicago, 94
  and Poor People's Campaign,
    90, 92–94, 95–96, 101–102
  and strike of black hospital
    workers in Charleston, South
    Carolina, 103–104
  and voter registration drives,
    66, 69, 74, 88–89
Soviet-American Women's
  Summit, and Coretta as
  cochair, 114
Spelman College (Atlanta), and
  Martin's casket in Sister's
  Chapel before funeral, 10

Spring Street School (Atlanta),
  Coretta's children in, 89–90
Story of the Struggle from 1955 to
  1965, The, 86
Stride Toward Freedom (Martin
  Luther King, Jr.), 66–67
Student Nonviolent Coordinating
  Committee (SNCC), 70, 95
Supreme Court
  and Brown v. Board of Education,
    48–49, 81
  and Montgomery bus boycott,
    60, 61, 62

Tennessee. See Memphis,
  Tennessee
Thurmond, Strom, 110
Treichler, Jessie, 29, 34
Tutu, Desmond, 115

United Nations
  and Coretta as public delegate,
    107
  and Coretta speaking at Inter-
    national Day of Solidarity
    with Women of South Africa
    and Namibia, 114
U.S. Justice Department, and
  Martin's assassination, 117
U.S. National Park Service, and
  Martin's home and neighbor-
  hood as historic district, 110
Universal Love Award, Coretta
  receiving, 103

Vietnam War, Coretta and
  Martin against, 43, 101
voter registration drives
  in Albany, Georgia, 74
  and Coretta, 66, 69, 85, 87, 89
  and march from Selma to
    Montgomery, 88–89

in Marion, Alabama, 87–89
and Martin, 66, 69, 74, 85
in Montgomery, Alabama, 69
in Selma, Alabama, 87–88
Voting Rights Act, 89, 90

Wallace, George, 77, 88, 89
Washington, D.C.
  and March on Washington for Jobs and Freedom, 81, 83, 110
  and Poor People's Campaign, 95–96, 101–102
Washington Post, 106, 107
Watts riot, 95
"We Shall Overcome" (song), 70, 111
Williams, Hosea, 8
Williams, Mary Lucy, 57
Williams, Olive, 21
Wittenberg, University of, 92

Women for a Meaningful Summit, Coretta heading delegation of, 114
Women Mobilized for Change, Coretta involved with, 93
Women Strike for Peace, Coretta in Geneva with, 73–75
Women's Day programs, Coretta speaking at, 66, 69
Women's International League for Peace and Freedom, Coretta joining, 69
Wonder, Stevie, 110

Young, Andrew
  on Coretta's activism, 106
  and Martin's assassination, 2–3, 8
  in Norway for Martin's Nobel Peace Prize, 87
  and Southern Christian Leadership Conference, 10

page:

5: © Flip Schulke/CORBIS
8: Associated Press
12: © Bettmann/CORBIS
15: Schomburg Center for
Research in Black Culture,
New York Public Library,
Ashton, Lennox, and
Tilden Foundation
23: Library of Congress,
LC-USZ62-116824
26: Antiochiana, Olive
Kettering Library
31: Antiochiana, Olive
Kettering Library
35: New England Conservatory
of Music

41: © Flip Schulke/CORBIS
46: © Bettmann/CORBIS
53: Associated Press, AP
59: Associated Press, AP/
Gene Herrick
67: Associated Press, AP
75: Associated Press, AP
78: © Flip Schulke/CORBIS
82: Associated Press, AP
91: © Flip Schulke/CORBIS
97: Associated Press, AP/
Charles Kelly
100: © Bettmann/CORBIS
111: © CORBIS
115: © Reuters/CORBIS
118: Associated Press, AP/Ric Feld

Cover: © William Coupon/CORBIS

ABOUT THE AUTHOR

Lisa Renee Rhodes is a graduate of Bernard M. Baruch College, City University of New York, and the Columbia Graduate School of Journalism. She is a writer and reviewer of literature for children and young adults.

AUTHOR OF ADDITIONAL TEXT, LEGACY EDITION

Dale Evva Gelfand has worked in publishing for some 25 years as a writer and editor. She is the author of a number of books about nature and gardening—including *Grow a Hummingbird Garden, A Little Book of Flowers*, and *Creating Habitat for Backyard Birds*—as well as a contributing writer for books on women's health and child raising. She recently put her love of medieval history to good use by authoring *Charlemagne* for Chelsea House. When not reading basically anything she can get her hands on, she can be found planting gardens, hiking through the woods, and photographing the natural world.

CONSULTING EDITOR, REVISED EDITION

Heather Lehr Wagner is a writer and editor. She is the author of 30 books exploring social and political issues and focusing on the lives of prominent Americans and has contributed to biographies of *Alex Haley, Langston Hughes, Colin Powell*, and *Jesse Owens*, in the BLACK AMERICANS OF ACHIEVEMENT legacy series. She earned a BA in political science from Duke University and an MA in government from the College of William and Mary. She lives with her husband and family in Pennsylvania.

CONSULTING EDITOR, FIRST EDITION

Nathan Irvin Huggins was W.E.B. Du Bois Professor of History and Director of the W.E.B. Du Bois Institute for Afro-American Research at Harvard University. He previously taught at Columbia University. Professor Huggins was the author of numerous books, including *Black Odyssey: The Afro-American Ordeal in Slavery, The Harlem Renaissance*, and *Slave and Citizen: The Life of Frederick Douglass.* Nathan I. Huggins died in 1989.